JOSEPH CORVO'S
ZONE
THERAPY

JOSEPH CORVO'S
ZONE
THERAPY

Youth, beauty and health in ten minutes a day

ARROW

A Vermilion Arrow Book

First published in Great Britain
in 1990 by Century
This revised edition published
in 1993 by Vermilion Arrow
an imprint of Ebury Press
Random House
20 Vauxhall Bridge Road
London SW1V 2SA

1 3 5 7 9 10 8 6 4 2

Illustrations by Robin Harris/Inklink
Photographs by Trevor Leighton

A catalogue record for this book is available from the
British Library

Filmset in Plantin Light by SX Composing Ltd.,
Rayleigh, Essex
Printed and bound in Great Britain by
Cox & Wyman Ltd., Reading, Berkshire

ISBN 0 09 923021 6

CONTENTS

A MESSAGE FROM JOSEPH CORVO

Press away the years. Press away pain and tiredness. Press away illness. Zone Therapy is the complete programme for youth, beauty and health. With Zone Therapy a 70-year-old can have the youth and health of a 50-year-old, a 60-year-old can have the youth and health of a 40-year-old, a 40-year-old can look and feel like a 30-year-old. Zone Therapy is absolutely safe. There is nothing complicated about the system laid out in this book. Anyone can do it and achieve results. Use Zone Therapy and you need never be sick. If you are already sick, use Zone Therapy and you will be amazed. All you have to do is to apply pressure to the correct spot. This book will show you how to do this.

Always consult your physician for any persistent disorder, but you will find that Zone Therapy will complement any treatment your physician gives you. Just follow the instructions and you will be astounded at the results.

Joseph Corvo

INTRODUCTION

Congratulations! You have entered into the wonderful world of perfect bodies. I am going to tell you how to achieve a state free from the distresses of old age, pain and ugliness. From this day forward you are going to progress until your body is a wonderful thing to behold. By reading this book and putting into practice what you read, you will improve yourself physically and mentally. You will never look back. You are entering a new phase.

Having practised this form of treatment for nearly thirty years, I can tell you it works. The many thousands of patients I have treated include royalty, politicians, top business people and show-business celebrities. Now I want everyone, not just the rich and famous, to benefit from my treatment.

You can shed years. Beauty is yours for the asking. In Britain alone there are 7½ million registered arthritics, and forty-six million working days are lost through back pain; ninety-five per cent of these are unnecessary, because back pain can be successfully treated through Zone Therapy. Abnormal organs can be normalized; eyesight can be corrected; deaf ears can often be made to hear; weak livers and kidneys, and faulty adrenals, all respond to Zone Therapy. When this form of healing is finally understood, it will open up fields never before thought of and a new way of living will emerge.

It is, in my opinion, God's treatment. The human being is the most wonderful creation of all time. Think of the Infinite Intelligence that created humankind. For everything that goes wrong with you, there exists within you, by Divine

Providence, a mechanism for correcting that malfunction. I believe that God, in His wisdom, put such a system into our bodies. By activating this system certain charismatic individuals have practised healing since the beginning of time. They have been known as miracle-workers. Only now are we beginning to understand how this system and this healing works. Now you too can have miracle hands.

From the moment you start practising Zone Therapy on yourself, or on your family, you must *believe* in youth, good health, happiness and well-being. Follow the instructions for the rest of your life and believe in them and you will enjoy the kind of youth, health and beauty you never thought possible; all of these beyond your wildest dreams.

I ask only that you practise my instructions to the letter. If I indicate two minutes' pressure don't do five minutes' pressure. If I tell you to practise every day I mean every day and not once a week.

There is nothing difficult or complicated about it. Everything is explained simply. You can treat yourself. Husband can treat wife, wife can treat husband and both can treat the children. Boyfriend can treat girlfriend, and vice versa. Whatever the situation, treatment can be self-administered or given with complete confidence without any need for special training other than reading this book and following my instructions. Great care has been taken in the description of zones and the precise way in which to apply pressure together with the use of simple tools such as rubber bands, clothes pegs and combs.

Think of the millions who go jogging, play tennis, do body building and other varied forms of exercise. These are all excellent in themselves but, sadly, unless your internal parts such as glands, organs and the nervous system are receiving the same dedicated attention, then sports and physical exercise can only take you halfway on the quest for perfect health. You are, indeed, only what your inner mechanics allow you to be. Exercise should be backed up by the equally important exercise of all these mechanics, and it is only Zone Therapy which can reach the important key centres. With Zone Therapy you can work every gland and organ in your body up to 100 per cent capacity. In the 1990s Zone Therapy will be the thinking person's approach to health and beauty. I give you health and beauty from within.

So with Zone Therapy you need never be ill or feel old. All it takes is a session of ten minutes' duration per day and careful attention to the diet details provided. The aim of this book is to help you achieve LIFE. LIFE is a very hard quality to define. You can almost feel it as well as see and hear it. It includes many qualities such as sparkling eyes, grace, attractive movements of the fingers, hands, head and body. It can also include such incidentals as the mannerisms of lifting an eyebrow or the position of the legs when standing, an intimate voice or a catchy accent. LIFE as a quality is well understood by advertising experts. It is the elusive attraction that we see certain manufacturers trying to portray on our television screens.

We all know the scene: the hero, when pouring his drink or filling his pipe, has the eyes of a beautiful woman on him. Does he have this quality of LIFE? Their eyes meet: does *she* have this quality of LIFE? How do you rate? Anyone who is willing to search for the truth will find that with comparatively little effort, immense returns of strength, knowledge and peace result. It is all here waiting for you.

1

ALL ABOUT ZONE THERAPY

ZONE THERAPY AND ME

I was born in Yorkshire and brought up in a little village called Hickleton. My father worked down the mines. He couldn't afford to pay for my continuing education so, at the age of fourteen, I went down the mine too. A year later I won a singing competition and so began a career as a tenor. It was while on a concert tour of the States that I met Franz Henbach. He was a disciple of William Fitzgerald of Boston City Hospital, the Central London Hospital, and St Francis Hospital, Hartford, Connecticut, and who in the early years of the century tried to discover if there was any scientific basis for traditional oriental therapy such as reflexology. He correlated all his findings, and in so doing devised a wonderful new healing system, which he called Zone Therapy. I had had an interest in healing from the age of seven, when I used to heal my mother and friends of headaches and so on by massage. Now I was glad to learn from Franz Henbach a thinking, systematic approach. I became a disciple myself and began to learn the theory behind the practice.

I have been practising Zone Therapy for thirty years now – longer than anyone else – and have become the world's most famous practitioner. My world-wide reputation has been built on results. Royalty, film stars, top businessmen and politicians come to me, many through the recommendation of Barbara Cartland. She writes: 'Joseph Corvo is unique and a phenomenon. When I first met Joseph, having been told about him by The Duke of Abercorn, I realized at once he was different from anyone I had ever met. What he does is to make one physically well, and also to lift one specifically. I am more grateful than I can ever say for having found him.'

THE SCIENTIFIC BASIS OF ZONE THERAPY

Unlike other systems, such as acupuncture, Zone Therapy is grounded in medical science. There is some correlation between the thinking behind reflexology and Zone Therapy, but beside Zone Therapy reflexology is child's play.

THE ZONES

Science tells us that the body is an electromagnetic field, with electromagnetic currents coursing round it. Ten main invisible electrical currents run through the body in line with the toes and fingers. The area that each current covers is called a zone. The body is divided into equal parts with five zones on the left side and five on the right.

All organs, glands and nervous systems fall into these zones.

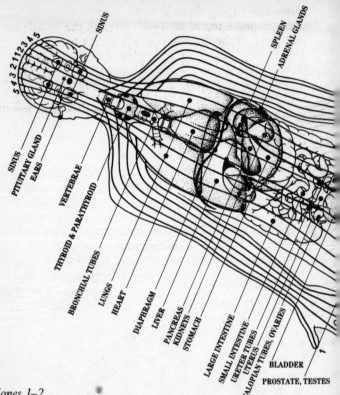

SINUS

SPLEEN

ADRENAL GLANDS

5 4 3 2 1 1 2 3 4 5

PITUITARY GLAND

SINUS

EARS

VERTEBRAE

THYROID & PARATHYROID

BRONCHIAL TUBES

LUNGS

HEART

DIAPHRAGM

LIVER

PANCREAS

KIDNEYS

STOMACH

LARGE INTESTINE

SMALL INTESTINE

URETER TUBES

UTERUS

FALOPIAN TUBES; OVARIES

BLADDER

PROSTATE, TESTES

1

Zones 1–2

come from the top of the head, run down through the centre of the forehead and nose and onwards through the centre of the body, branching off to the thumbs and big toes.

Zones 3–4

come from the top of the head, run down through the eye and onwards through the body to the first fingers and second toes.

Zones 5–6

come from the top of the head, through the eyes and down to the second fingers and third toes.

Zones 7–8
come from the top of the head, through the middle ear and down to the third fingers and fourth toes.

Zones 9–10
come from the top of the head, take in the external ear and continue down to the little or fourth fingers and fifth toes.

The areas on the hands and feet correspond to each other, thus:
the big toes and the thumbs are part of Zones 1 and 2;
the first fingers and second toes are part of Zones 3 and 4;
the middle or second fingers and third toes are part of Zones 5 and 6;
the third fingers and fourth toes are part of Zones 7 and 8;
the fourth or little fingers and fifth toes are part of Zones 9 and 10.

THE GLANDS

Youth, beauty and health depend above all else on the proper functioning of the glands. The endocrine glands are the rejuvenation glands of the body, for once they start to deteriorate we begin to age very quickly. The glands which make up the endocrines are the pituitary, the penial, the thyroids, the parathyroids, the thymus, the adrenals, the pancreas and the gonads.

THE PITUITARY

This is situated at the base of the brain, just above the back of the throat. It is encased in a long cradle of great strength to give it protection. It secretes hormones that activate and control the other important glands of the body. Because it controls the linear growth of the body, an overactive pituitary gland can produce a giant and an under-active pituitary can produce a very small person. As a result of imbalance in the pituitary, the thyroid gland will suffer and, eventually, the pancreas, adrenals, liver and kidneys will start to malfunction.

THE THYROIDS

The thyroids are situated on either side of the windpipe and produce thyroxine, a hormone which contains iodine. Thyroxine, the hormone, pours into the blood and is carried to all parts of the body. It tells the body cells to burn the amount of food necessary, and to produce the amount of energy needed to maintain the body at the required temperature. This greatly assists the heart action, and normal circulation to the entire system is attained.

If insufficient iodine is supplied, not enough thyroxine will be produced. The body then becomes sluggish, the heartbeat is lowered, breathing becomes somewhat laboured, constipation and bad digestion occur and a great lack of energy is felt. You become what people call lazy. You have no endurance. You feel cold quickly. You start to put

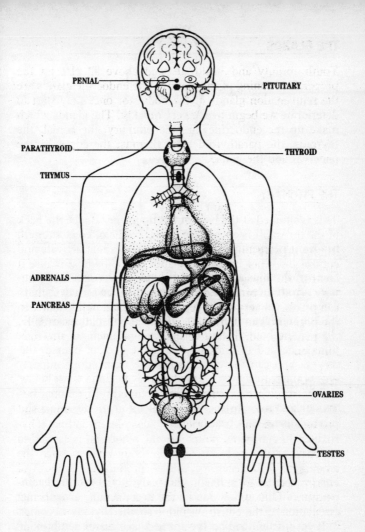

PENIAL

PITUITARY

PARATHYROID

THYROID

THYMUS

ADRENALS

PANCREAS

OVARIES

TESTES

on weight. Circulation is very poor. The skin can become dry and scaly. The hair has no life and can fall out by the handful. The memory suffers. Menstruation is unstable. You feel uncomfortable and distressed and very low in spirit. And, of course, unhappy.

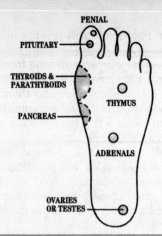

PENIAL

PITUITARY

THYROIDS &
PARATHYROIDS

THYMUS

PANCREAS

ADRENALS

OVARIES
OR TESTES

THE PARATHYROIDS

The parathyroids are situated behind the thyroid. The hormones from these glands circulate in the blood when there is a need for calcium and phosphorus. The parathyroids see that the correct amounts of calcium and phosphorus are supplied to the body during its life span. Remember that calcium is needed to relax muscle tissue and, of course, the nerves. You can therefore realize the tremendous importance of the parathyroids, for when they begin to work below par the result will eventually be excitability, irrational behaviour and nervousness. This will automatically affect the heart, causing it to beat faster.

THE THYMUS

The thymus gland is in the chest, slightly above the heart. During childhood this gland helps in controlling growth and development. As we grow older so the thymus becomes smaller. Could this be the gland that creates senility? It could well be so. The thymus does begin to shrink rapidly through chronic illness and great physical stress.

There is no doubt that it has an enormous effect on the immunity mechanisms of the body and that where the thymus is in a poor state it is much easier for serious infection to thrive. A condition like cancer will prosper in such an environment.

Patients I have treated who are suffering from shock, unhappiness, emotional and spiritual distress always show tremendous reaction to treatment over the thymus gland. I know then that kindness, understanding, confidence and inspiration are needed. After a few treatments, a considerable change takes place within the thymus.

Someday we shall know the full truth and facts about the thymus. To me it is the 'sun' of the glandular system surrounded by its planets, the pituitary gland, the thyroids, the liver, the pancreas, the kidneys, the adrenals and the prostate gland. I believe that most of the health troubles we have spring from the condition of the thymus.

If you are given any adverse news or you suffer even minor upsets, the effect upon the thymus is instant. As we all know, if the sun in the galaxy we live in altered in any way then the effect upon the earth would be very significant; what is less obvious is that you are a microcosm of the system you live in. When the thymus is affected in even the slightest degree, you automatically lose energy and the power within you diminishes accordingly. The more distress, shock, grief or illness you suffer, the less energy you obtain. If you think negatively or despairingly, the thymus is affected and you become distressed. On the other hand, if you think positively and encouragingly with good, beautiful thoughts, this will induce the thymus to give out tremendous energy. There is a rise in the level of adrenalin in the body and you feel strong.

THE ADRENALS

The adrenal glands are situated above the kidneys and secrete the hormone adrenalin. They are known as the glands of 'fight and flight'. When we experience anger or fear, large amounts of the hormone rush into the blood and prepare the body for action. Adrenalin creates a condition which causes the starch and glycogen stores in the liver and muscles to turn to sugar, thereby providing energy for immediate action. The adrenal glands always secrete a certain amount of adrenalin, causing glycogen to be turned into sugar when needed. A deficiency of adrenalin creates a condition of slowness and the inability to get clear when danger threatens.

THE PANCREAS

The pancreas is situated below the stomach and it secretes a hormone called insulin. This helps the body to store sugar in the form of starch or glycogen. Sugar is burnt to produce energy. As food is digested, the sugar flows into the bloodstream. Insulin is then secreted from the pancreas, and the liver and the muscles can take the sugar not immediately needed for energy from the blood and store it.

If the pancreas is in a state of malfunction, the correct amount of insulin can no longer be produced. The result is that sugar builds up in the blood and is passed out of the body during urination. Because the sugar should be used for energizing the body, a great loss of energy is the obvious consequence. Abnormalities begin to appear, the most common being diabetes, a most debilitating condition. If the pancreas is working correctly, this cannot happen.

THE GONADS

The health of the sex glands is very important to all men and women, for if they cease to function properly impotence, lack of sex drive and lack of control can result. Over the years I have treated many cases involving these glands. I have found the pituitary, the thyroids, the adrenals, the kidneys, the bladder and the prostate all in a state of malfunction. It takes time and patience to rectify this condition. You must be determined to carry on until you succeed.

ZONE THERAPY AGAINST TOXINS

The theory of Zone Therapy is that because of the toxic substances eaten, drunk or breathed in, crystalline deposits form around the terminal nerve endings. These deposits choke and prevent the electrical contact of the nerves from grounding, impeding the flow of the electromagnetic currents around the body. Illness then occurs because the balance of the electromagnetic field of the body is severely upset – that is, the amount of power flowing through a zone of the body is cut to a bare minimum; in this condition glands in that zone will start to deteriorate rapidly. When you practise Zone Therapy you are applying pressure over the appropriate nerve endings, so that the crystalline deposits are rubbed out. The nerves are then able to ground, and so the electromagnetic currents are enabled to flow freely again – glands and organs function healthily.

All ageing and illness is caused by a lessening of the electromagnetic currents. Zone Therapy stops them from lessening. If you practise zonal treatment whilst you are healthy you will never be sick. You need not age further. If you are already sick do not just rely on drugs but also practise Zone Therapy. Most drugs remove the symptoms without removing the cause, which in the long run only builds disease. Only Zone Therapy removes the cause.

As well as teaching you to heal I will also tell you how to get rid of bad habits that cause the build-up of harmful deposits around the terminal nerve endings. Look at the diseases brought on by TOXIN poisoning: diseases of the liver, diseases of the digestive system, diseases of the kidneys, arthritic diseases, diseases of the circulatory system, diseases of the blood, diseases of the ductless glands, nervous diseases and many others. TOXEMIA is a world-wide derangement and everywhere you go you can see its manifestations. The cure is in the correcting of the lifestyle of each and every individual.

From the moment you are born, you start to poison yourself. Therefore, unless you are regularly decongested you can imagine the amount of poisoning you must put into your own body in the course of the years. Is it any wonder that people end up with sickness?

Sadly, people are walking around today incubating disease within their own bodies. But if Zone Therapy were practised regularly, millions could enjoy full, rich lives instead of misery and despair. If the nervous systems, the glandular systems and the organs of the body are kept in perfect condition through the blood being purified by the elimination of poisons at regular intervals, sickness would be cut down to a bare minimum.

THE INSTINCT TO TOUCH

Zone Therapy, which is a technique of touching, is as old as the human race – you were born with it.

If you bang your head against a door, the first thing you do is to put your hand over the painful part and press it, because you instinctively feel the comfort coming from such an action. If you hit your thumb with a hammer, after cursing the next thing you do is to grab hold of the thumb and hold it very tightly. You are applying pressure again to give comfort. The need to pressurize parts of your body at certain times is born within you; your subconscious knows that pressure eases.

All through the ages there have been people who knew of this treatment and who were looked upon as miracle-workers because they were able to do what ordinary people apparently could not. They were able to touch a person, give a little bit of pressure, and the pain would disappear.

Now I am going to teach you how and where to touch in order to heal. Now you too can be a miracle-worker.

YOUTH, BEAUTY AND HEALTH

Remember that this physical body of yours is the only one you are going to have. You must make sure that it is kept in condition. Are you as youthful as you could be? Are you as attractive as it is possible to be? Is your skin clear and are your eyes shining? Is your hair lustrous?

Do not be satisfied with yourself until you radiate health and beauty. Beauty is the result of inner health and this comes from constant repair work on the zones of your body.

Make up your mind that you are going to possess the most beautiful body, that you are going to radiate health, happiness and beauty. Work at it for ten minutes a day and before your very eyes the transformation will take place.

JOSEPH CORVO'S FACE PLAN

INCLUDING THE TEN-MINUTE MIRACLE

Your face is the most important part of your anatomy because it is the only part of you which is constantly on display. By far the largest part of our lives is spent fully clothed and friends and strangers judge us by what they see – THE FACE.

When attending for a job or business interview your face is under close observation and your capabilities and character are largely judged by what your face reflects. And the chances are that when you meet a potential friend or lover, male or female, your face will play a large part in the operation, so let's give the face a little care.

The face mirrors our emotions, conveys our thoughts and is the first thing people notice and like or dislike about us. Since your face is composed of muscles, skin and nerves, just like the rest of your body, has it ever occurred to you that by giving a little attention to it your face can become firmer, fuller and more handsome and beautiful?

THE NATURAL FACE-LIFT

This beauty programme is unlike any you have seen before. It is based on the system of Zone Therapy. It is easy and safe. The results will astonish you.

By doing the exercises and by massaging certain pressure points in the way I am going to teach you, you will first stimulate the muscle tissue lying below the surface. This is an essential step in improving your skin tone. Spare a few minutes each day and treatment will help you achieve a beautiful facial appearance with the velvety look of health. Also, and even more important, because of the structure of the body's electromagnetic fields, the massage points shown on the facial chart affect areas other than your face. In fact, your whole being will respond to this unique treatment, health problems can be overcome, and you will experience a sense of elation and well-being.

With this programme, you can create beauty externally and internally.

So the happy truth of the matter is that by a little local exercise on the face itself, it can be kept looking young, strong, handsome, beautiful, well into old age. It is a matter of muscular tone and an augmental circulation of the blood. While the bone structure of the skull has a lot to do with the shape of your face, we can also consider the fact that the face is composed of thick layers of muscle which can be greatly changed and improved in size and shape, just as the muscles of the body can be changed and improved.

The chin can be made larger, rounder and stronger in appearance. The jaw line can be made straighter and more firm, the lips can be much improved in shape and lines from nose to mouth and hollows under the eyes can be filled out. Facial exercise may also greatly improve the complexion, and pimples, blackheads and enlarged pores may be helped. The mouth can also be improved in shape and its expressions brought under control through exercise. The mouth is a large circular muscle with a hole in the middle. It is very flexible, stretching to an opening the size of an orange and contracting to the size of a pea. When this muscle is well exercised the lips become full and expressive in conversation. When not cared for the mouth muscle will show every bit of strain and nervous tension the body is subjected to. The lips will be tight and colourless and there may be little lines running from the nose to the corners of the mouth.

The muscles around the eyes also respond to exercise, as do the forehead, cheeks and chin. The muscles around the eyes are closely connected with the nervous system and, since the skin is very thin in this area, nervous reaction brought on by strain, worry or loss of sleep is easily seen.

Irritated nerves eat up fatty tissue and when we dissipate it is this loss of fat under the thin skin around the eyes that makes those telltale hollows, dark circles and bags. Facial exercise may help control this loss of fatty tissue. Carefully compare the appearance of young eyes and of old; you will find the difference is largely due to the full layer of flesh under the skin in youth, and the lack of it in the aged. You can help retain this layer of flesh by exercise and augmented circulation which will help you to keep your eyes young-looking.

People who end up having cosmetic or plastic surgery usually do so because they have lost all of the muscle tissue in the face and neck and see no alternative. This is what The Joseph Corvo Face Plan is all about: helping you with your muscles for, if you lose your face muscles, you lose your looks.

Follow my plan and you will look young, handsome and beautiful.

Exercise one

The first exercise is to start puckering the lips as though to whistle, making the hole as small as possible and forcing the lips far forward as though trying to touch an object a few inches in front of the face. At the same time close the eyes, pulling all the muscles forward towards the mouth, and continue to pucker the lips and force them far forward. Hold this contraction intensely for twenty seconds.

Exercise two

Now relax and go immediately into the opposite movement. Stretch the eyes wide open and raise the eyebrows. Open your mouth and stretch it to the utmost limit; concentrate on forcing everything away from the mouth. Continue to stretch the mouth wider and pull all the muscles outwards with all your might. Hold this contraction for twenty seconds, then continue by repeating exercises 1 and 2 alternately for a period of two minutes.

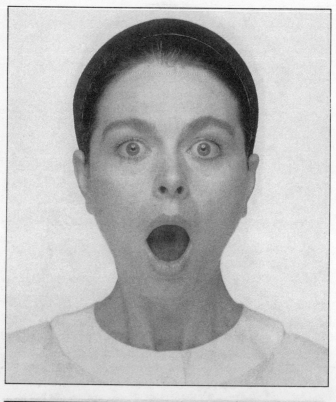

Exercise three

Next, keeping the teeth closed tight, force the chin muscle down with all your willpower and hold it there, trying to keep the upper part of your face relaxed. Now force the chin muscle upward and hold. After you have learned to control this movement try a brisker routine. Do four very slowly and eight fast. In what will seem a few seconds, your chin will ache from the effort and very soon you will see a marked improvement in the size and contour of your chin. A strong chin improves anyone's face. This exercise will help you make the most of yours.

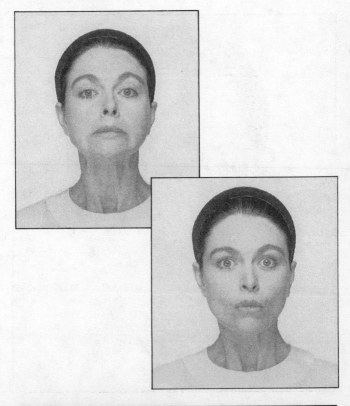

Exercise four

Here is an exercise to build muscles into your throat and neck. Tip your head back as if looking at the ceiling. Now place your right hand in the centre of your forehead as you try to bring your head back to a level keel. Resist with your right hand so that you have to force your hand down if you bring your head level again. Do this exercise six times in a row.

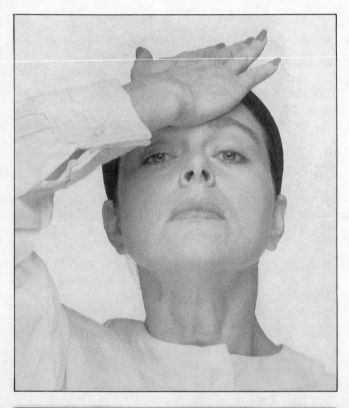

Exercise five

Drop your head on to your chest. Put your right hand at the back of your head. Now force your head back up off your chest to its normal level, all the time resisting with your right hand. Practise six times to begin with then start to alternate exercise 5 with exercise 4 and just watch the muscles on your neck and throat build up.

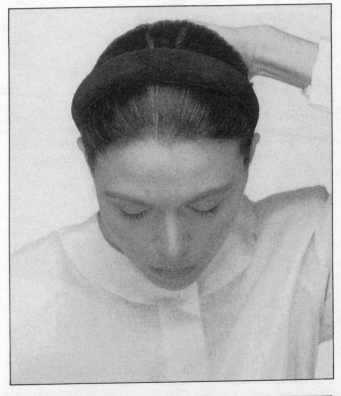

Exercise six

Puff out your cheeks and squeeze your mouth to the size of a pea. Then give your face a good vigorous slapping for two minutes. Just slap your face – it will do wonders for you.

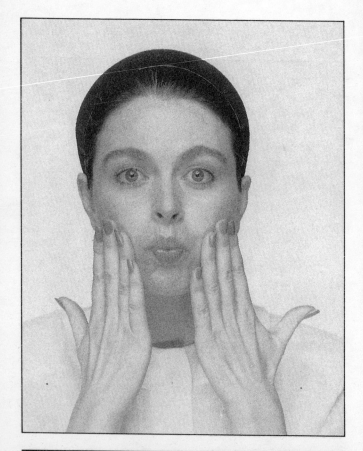

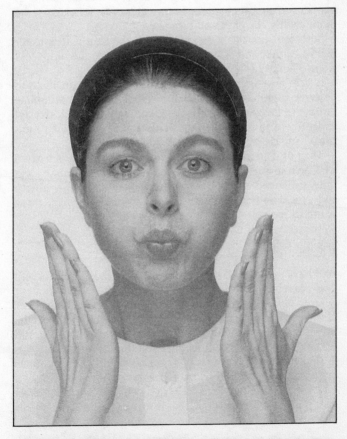

FACIAL MASSAGE

When our nerve endings become blocked and choked, the amount of electromagnetic power flowing through the body is severely restricted and all organs become damaged, including the largest one, the skin. Not enough blood, oxygen, protein and minerals reach the face. Dry and flaccid skin appears. Sometimes the muscles of the face will literally waste away and loose skin will hang from the bone structure. The longer the 'blocking' process continues (and this happens to almost everyone to a greater or lesser extent), the more swiftly the skin and face age.

Sufficient nourishment must reach the skin if it is to remain healthy, and if new cells are to replace the old. Only Zone Therapy can ensure this nourishment.

A firm massage on key points of the face, as I am about to describe, will help to free the nerve endings, stimulate muscle tissue and allow adequate supplies of blood, oxygen and protein to reach the face. This will at once start to improve muscle building and skin tone.

Most of us don't realize that we lose our good looks when we lose our muscle tissue. Yet the remedy is so simple. It is fully explained in the following pages. Follow this advice and you won't need a face-lift to achieve a fresher, more youthful look.

THE TECHNIQUES OF TOUCHING

As I have said, we all have an instinctive need to care for and heal ourselves by touch, but we don't know exactly how or where. This is what I am now going to teach you. The zones of the body vary slightly in position in each individual so the pressure points I give you in the charts and in the text and photographs are approximate. If you don't find it exactly as in the chart and photograph, either go slightly below, above or to the side and you will contact the right point; you will be able to tell when you have done this because the exact spot for you will be the one that is sore and sensitive – this is because of the toxins you have accumulated there.

Make certain that your nails are cut short so that you don't lacerate your skin. Use the top joint of the thumb. Place the top of the thumb over the point indicated in the diagram and press into the area, rotating in a clockwise motion or anticlockwise motion, whichever you like, as long as you remember to use a rotating movement. You can use the fingertips in the same way.

Always massage with an upward and outward circular movement. You can work quite deeply on the various pressure points with a very firm action. Remember you are breaking down the toxins blocking your nerve endings to allow blood and oxygen to reach your face. (The exceptions are pressure points 3, 4 and 15, where you must use a more gentle massage movement.)

Some people can take more pressure than others. For all points apart from 3, 4 and 15, press as hard as you can without feeling uncomfortable. You will find your own level by what you feel. Where there is deep congestion it will be

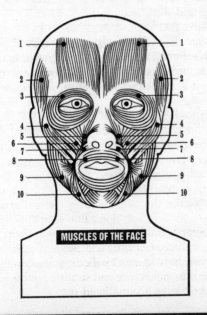

MUSCLES OF THE FACE

1 FRONTALIS
2 TEMPORAL
3 OCULI
4 ZYGOMATIC
5 LEVATOR LABII SUPERIORES
  ET ALAE NASI
6 LEVATOR LABII SUPERIORES
7 DEPRESSOR ALAE NASI
8 ORBICULARIS ORIS
9 DEPRESSOR ANGULI ORIS
10 DEPRESSOR LABII INFERIORES

tender and you will be able to bear less pressure, so use your common sense and don't work at it too vigorously. Over a period of time you will be able to massage more deeply as you remove the condition. And after a series of treatments you will break down the crystalline deposits and completely free all the systems, enabling them to return to normal activity.

I repeat: do not apply consistent pressure for long periods over hurtful spots. Give painful areas a few seconds' pressure, then move on and come back to the tender places after a short rest.

In fact Zone Therapy is usually quite painful in many areas in the beginning, but, over a period of time, as you eliminate poison from the particular nerve ending and stimulate the gland, the painful areas will decrease, until eventually there is no tenderness left in that particular area. When you have done that, you know you have done a good job!

TEN MINUTES EVERY DAY

It doesn't matter at what time of day you carry out the treatment, but it is important to do it regularly. Just imagine: in ten minutes, as well as giving your complexion the attention it surely deserves, you have helped to tone up your entire system.

Now we will go on to the VITAL PRESSURE POINTS on your face to get your face and body under your control.

How to massage your face

First wash or cleanse your face and dry it thoroughly. Then refer to the face chart and accompanying photographs, and start to work on each pressure point in turn, beginning with number 1 and continuing to number 15. Spend about thirty seconds on each pressure point.

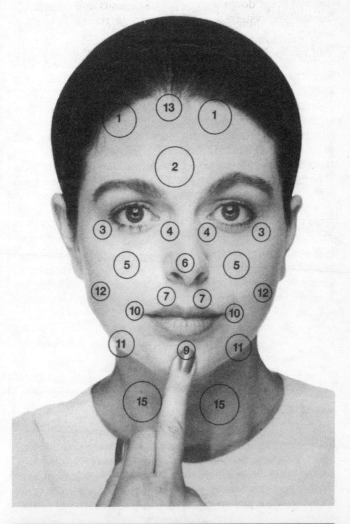

IMPROVING THE FOREHEAD AND MENTAL ALERTNESS

Surprisingly enough, massaging these areas can actually improve your thinking processes and activate your reflexes. The pressure you exert also clears blockages in the nerve endings in the forehead, allowing more blood and oxygen to reach your skin and so purifying your face.

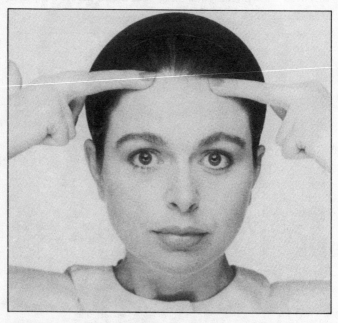

Exercise

Find the edge of the forehead, where the bone indents, then with a firm upward and outward circular movement of about half-an-inch radius slowly move both fingers in towards the centre of the forehead, then out again. Complete four times. Remember, if it is tender, that is because poisons are blocking the proper functioning of this zone in your body.

STIMULATING THE PITUITARY GLAND AND HORMONES

Pressure here stimulates the pituitary gland. This produces the hormones needed by the entire reproductive system. It is the master gland and should be kept in perfect working order. You will find to your astonishment that massaging this area will enliven your imagination and greatly improve your perception.

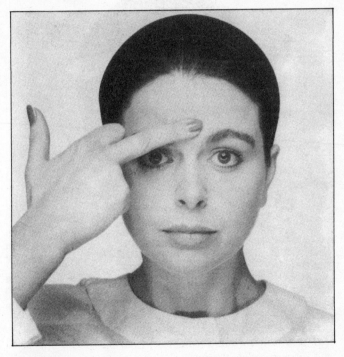

Exercise

Find the slight indent in your forehead. Massage again, upward and outward in a half-inch radius for thirty seconds.

FACIAL SKIN AND THE COLON

It is vital to keep the colon in good working order. If it begins to malfunction, poisons will build up internally because waste matter is not being eliminated properly. The appearance of the face will suffer accordingly.

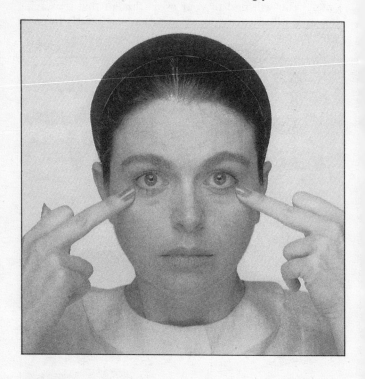

Exercise

To massage pressure points 3 and 4, tap gently underneath the eye, starting on the outside and moving inwards towards the nose, then out again. Complete four times.

ACTIVATING THE KIDNEYS TO BANISH TOXINS

Healthy kidneys eliminate toxins and acidity. As most of the food we eat has a good deal of acidity, it is easy to see how vital these organs are. Any abnormality will affect a person's general health and the skin on the face will suffer very badly.

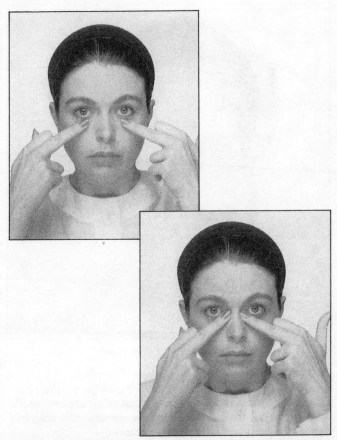

GLOWING SKIN AND THE DIGESTIVE PROCESS

Most of us don't think too much about our bowels. We should. Sluggish bowels are one of the main reasons for dull-looking, pasty skin. Massage the appropriate pressure points well.

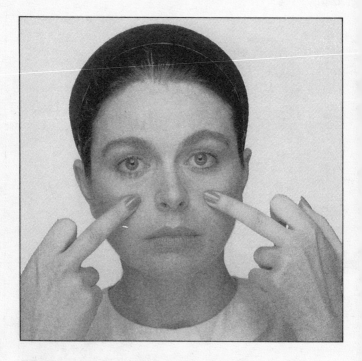

Exercise

Find the ridge of the cheekbone at its highest point, press up into it, then massage as hard as you can in an upward and outward circular movement, while moving slowly the length of the cheekbone. Complete four times.

THE IMPORTANCE OF THE STOMACH

Sufferers from digestive trouble may be surprised to learn that simply by massaging the tip of the nose vigorously their digestion will be greatly improved. It's all to do with blocked nerve endings again.

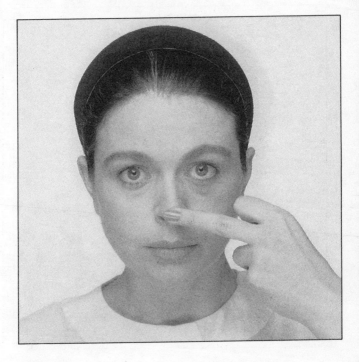

Exercise

Without lifting the fingers, slide along the skin of your nose, press as hard as you feel comfortable with and rotate slowly for thirty seconds.

HELPING THE SPLEEN REMOVE WORN-OUT BLOOD CELLS

A healthy spleen means a healthy stomach, so be sure to massage these areas thoroughly.

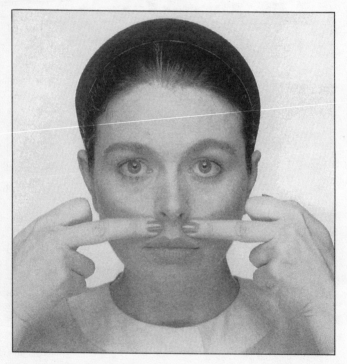

Exercise

Pressing inwards on either side of the ridge that runs from your nose to the middle of your upper lip, rotate your fingers in a half-inch radius. Press hard so that you feel your gums underneath.

THE PANCREAS AND HEALTHY SKIN TISSUE

This secretes alkaline enzymes which help the digestive process. A malfunction can cause too much acidity which is very harmful to the skin. So massaging these areas thoroughly can help to attain a beautiful skin and face.

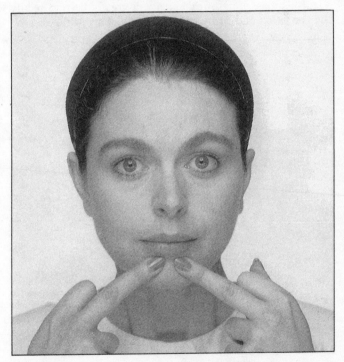

Exercise

Starting at the extremities of the underside of the lips, work inwards with a firm rotating motion towards the centre, then out again. Complete four times. Feel your lower gums through your lower lip.

BANISHING CONSTIPATION AND LACKLUSTRE SKIN

Sufferers from constipation will not need to be reminded what a problem it is. It's one of the main causes of sluggishness and lack of energy. A build-up of large amounts of toxins results in lacklustre skin and eyes and unpleasant breath. Vigorous massaging of this area will greatly help to rectify the condition and bring back life and colour to the face.

Exercise

Find the indent in your chin, then rotate your finger there as firmly as you can bear for thirty seconds.

STIMULATING THE LUNGS AND YOUR OXYGEN SUPPLY

Massaging this area will persuade the lungs to work better, helping to keep colds, bronchitis and asthma at bay. The better supply of oxygen resulting will improve not only the skin of the face but that of the whole body.

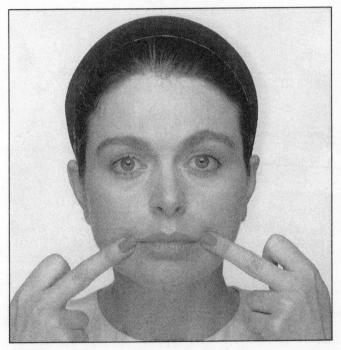

Exercise

Find the muscle running down the length of the side of the mouth, then press inwards and outwards with your rotating motion as hard as you can bear for thirty seconds.

INCREASING THE SEX DRIVE

The health of the sex glands is important to all of us. Their failure can bring impotence, lack of sex drive and lack of control. So it is advisable to massage these areas vigorously as they affect the entire reproductive system. The proper functioning of the sex glands brings a glow to face and skin.

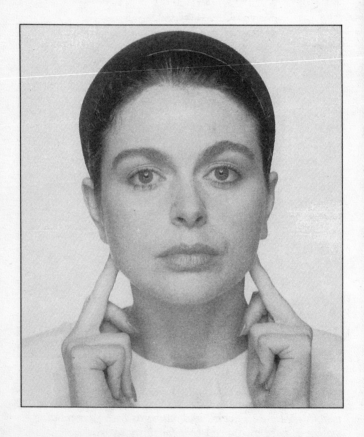

Exercise

Starting immediately below the ear, rub with your rotating movement along the ridge of the jawbone until your fingers are directly underneath the pupils of your eyes. Work back again and repeat four times as hard as you can.

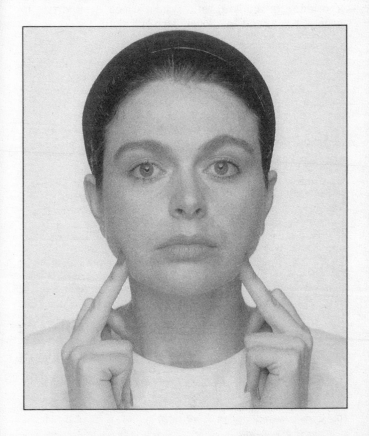

AIDING THE LIVER AND LYMPHATIC SYSTEM

For us to feel truly well and look really healthy it is vital to keep the liver in peak condition. A sluggish liver affects the entire body, especially the facial skin. The liver helps to purify the blood; impure blood means sagging skin and a face that looks older than it should. Massage in these areas also tones up the lymphatic system which is important to general health and to a lovely face and skin.

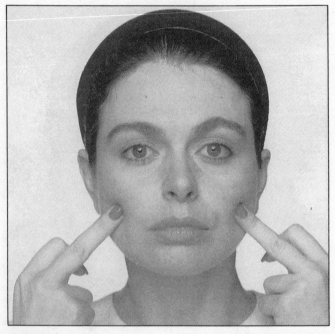

Exercise

Find the deepest pit of the cheek, where the jawbone meets the cheekbones. Work in a half-inch radius as hard as you can for thirty seconds.

TONING UP THE WHOLE NERVOUS SYSTEM

Massaging this area tones up the whole nervous system and brings a sense of peace and tranquillity. This feeling of well-being is always reflected in the face.

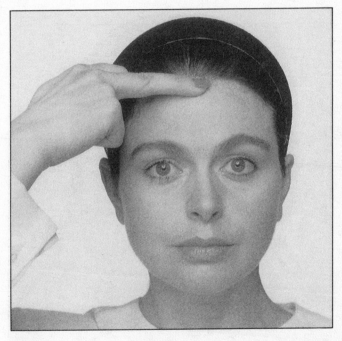

Exercise

Work the centre point high on your forehead in a half-inch radius as hard as you can for thirty seconds.

IMPROVING FACIAL MUSCLES AND YOUR ENTIRE
SYSTEM

Massage both ears in turn by taking the entire ear between
fingers and thumb. Start at the top and work down and up
as hard as you can four times. After a few minutes your
whole system will be pervaded by a glowing tingle. The
effect will be seen in the facial muscles and the general tone
of the face.

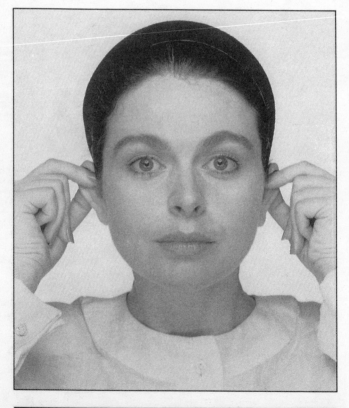

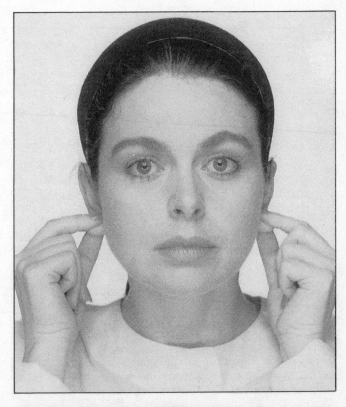

HELPING THE THYROIDS MAKE YOU FEEL GOOD

The thyroids are situated on either side of the windpipe. They are vital to good health for, if they fail to work properly, the body becomes sluggish, the heartbeat is lowered and breathing becomes laboured. Sufferers feel the cold intensely and may put on weight; their circulation is poor and their skin becomes dry and scaly. They may also be distressed and unhappy and suffer several other unwanted symptoms including poor memory and problems with menstruation. All this from the two little glands.

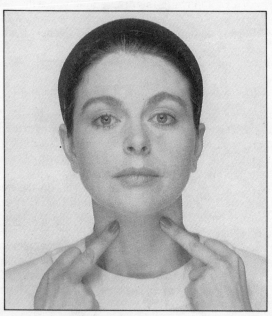

To avoid all these ills and enjoy beautiful skin, work gently but well over the thyroid glands. Starting either side of the thyroids, move inwards and upwards with a gentle circular movement. Complete four times.

If you follow the advice in this book and massage the various pressure points regularly you will give your face an entirely new and emollient look. Your muscle tissue and skin will firm up to become a natural 'face-lift'.

Because your whole body is being treated you will become beautiful outside and in. If overweight, you will notice a slimming effect around hips, thighs and stomach.

The Joseph Corvo Youth, Beauty and Health Programme. It's the treatment you always wanted but have never before found. Enjoy it. And be beautiful.

After many years of practical experience, I believe absolutely that by following the programme you will:

● feel fitter, younger, more energetic, livelier, healthier;

● have a more attractive face, a lovelier skin;

● reduce weight around hips, thighs, stomach.

There is a key which unlocks the doors to health, beauty and physical harmony – it is belief. Those who carefully follow my treatment will, I believe, release spiritual powers that encourage the attainment of true health, beauty and greater happiness. You must believe too.

As you practise my programme, as you do the massage, say to yourself, 'I am going to work until I am perfect'. Feel the natural powers you are releasing so that they can circulate freely and effectively within you; visualize your perfect, beautifully muscular self as it will be when you persist with Zone Therapy; believe that this is God's way of giving you freedom from the penalties of old age and disease. Be positive. Keep up your enthusiasm until success is yours.

DRINK WATER

After each session of ten minutes drink a glass of water. This will help flush out the toxins you have dislodged from the nerve endings.

CHAPTER 3

THE ZONE THERAPY DIET

Many of the diets I see advocated these days promote slimming at the expense of health, and most of them advise people to consume foods containing the very toxins Zone Therapy is designed to disperse. It is true that, generally speaking, the smaller your waistline, the longer your lifeline; nevertheless there is a grave risk of seriously damaging your health unless you diet within the context of a comprehensive health philosophy.

And this is what is unique about Zone Therapy. It is the most comprehensive health philosophy there is, because it shows you how to keep the inside of your body in the same excellent, 100 per cent healthy condition as the outside, and how to make inside and outside work in harmony. What could be more common-sensical? If you neglect the inside of your body in order to concentrate entirely on the outside, then of course interior decay will eventually cause your exterior to deteriorate too, and so all your dieting and exercising will prove to have been in vain.

So one of the great things about Zone Therapy is that it brings both extraordinarily rapid results and long-term benefits. Follow my dietary recommendations and not only will you lose weight more quickly than you could have imagined possible, but you can also count on 100 per cent health and greatly increased life expectancy.

I must emphasize, though, that this diet programme has been scientifically developed over many years to complement the Zone Therapy exercise regime, and that in order to achieve these results you must follow my diet in conjunction with your daily ten-minute pressure-point massage. I recommend that in particular you concentrate on toning up the endochrine system: the pituitary gland, the thyroids, the parathyroids, the thymus and the adrenals. These glands work together to control your body's conversion of food into electrical energy. If they are only working sluggishly, food will tend to be converted into fat rather than energy, so it is vital to get them working in harmony for maximum efficiency.

Practise the Zone Therapy 7-Day Diet. The results are miraculous!

SLENDER AND BEAUTIFUL

If you are overweight you have eaten more food than your body needs and the excess has become fat. Anyone with a normal bone structure can have as trim a body as he or she is willing to work for. You can remould your body with a diet of delicious but non-fattening foods.

The first step is to acquire a taste for these non-fattening foods by changing your eating habits. It is not the occasional heavy dinner or chocolate indulgence that causes you to put on weight; it is the types of food you eat day after day. What I call 'wallpaper-paste foods', such as white bread, refined cereals, cakes, pastries and biscuits, will have to be rejected. If you have given up taking sugar in tea and coffee, and lost the habit, you will know how horrible these drinks taste when you accidentally drink them sweetened with sugar. The same is true of all these fattening foods. You must learn to dislike them.

In fact, unless you are willing to learn, do not even bother to try the diet that follows, because no matter how many pounds you lose you will gain them again. Rather you should acquire the taste for low-calorie foods, and then your weight problem will be solved for the rest of your life. Not only that, but you are going to feel better than you have ever felt. You're going to look, feel and act as if you have been reborn.

Before I tell you about my 7-Day Diet, which you must repeat until you reach your perfect weight and which must be practised in conjunction with your daily Zone Therapy exercise programme, I wish to emphasize five vital dietary principles that should guild you throughout your life, even after you have achieved your ideal weight.

1 Don't forget that the process of digestion begins in the mouth. All your food must be very well chewed before you swallow it. So many people are in the habit of hurrying their meal and then washing it all down with a cup of coffee, with the result that an unmasticated, undigested mass lies in the stomach a long time, requiring considerable energy to break it down. You cannot afford to waste this energy, so give your teeth the work they were meant to do. All foods, including fluids, must be mixed with saliva in the mouth before swallowing.

2 Avoid all foods with no nutritional value, particularly those with a high-calorie content; I am, of course, referring again to refined sugar, sweets, pastries, cake, white bread etc. If you persist in eating these kinds of junk foods, you will undo much of the good work achieved by your daily practising of the Zone Therapy pressure-point massage programme.

3 The success of Zone Therapy's miraculous rejuvenating powers hinges on the rebuilding of muscles; therefore you must make sure you have a high protein intake. Neglect protein and muscles will fade away, leaving loose skin and wrinkles. The healthiest ways to take protein are:

● drinking yoghurt made from skimmed milk – the B vitamins made in your intestines by the yoghurt's bacteria will keep your skin in excellent condition: even if you are dieting I recommend a pint per day;

● eating the whites of two eggs or a ½ lb portion of lean meat or a good helping (2 tablespoonfuls) of cottage cheese: even if you are dieting you need to do this once a day;

● eating ¼ lb portions of either nuts or soya beans: nuts are fattening and should be avoided by those who are dieting, but soya beans can be eaten in moderation even on the strictest diet.

4 Zone Therapy's unique system of pressure-point massage is designed to bring your organs and glands to 100 per cent efficiency in processing vital vitamins and minerals, so it is important in your diet to eat these vitamins and minerals regularly and in the correct quantities. Whenever possible eat vegetables with a high vitamin and mineral content:

● Asparagus, Brussels sprouts, cabbage, carrots, cauliflower, celery, chard, courgettes, cucumber, eggplant, kale, leeks, lettuce, parsley, pumpkin, radishes, spinach, string beans, tomatoes

● Green and red peppers are especially high in vitamin C content while being low in calories, so get into the habit of eating them frequently. Put them in salads and in vegetable-juice cocktails.

Vegetable Juices

Juices extracted from fresh young vegetables are generally rich in goodness, making up for any vitamin or mineral deficiencies with extraordinary speed. They are also easily assimilated by people with weakened digestions. Often children who hate vegetables will down glasses of fresh vegetable juice with elfin delight, and they can be a joy to old people who have lost the ability to chew.

All the cocktails below can be made in any blender. Always select the youngest vegetables possible, and remember that though they should be cleaned they should not be peeled. Drink the juice fresh out of the extractor unless it needs to be chilled, in which case it should go straight in the fridge.

In order to maintain a high energy level, the following drinks should be taken at least twice a day between meals:

Carrot Juice

Trim the carrots and scrub them clean, then cut into pieces to fit the extractor. After blending, add a few drops of lemon or orange juice to help keep the colour as well as to enhance the taste.

Beetroot Juice

Trim, wash, cut up young beetroots for the juicing machine, then blend with canned pineapple juice in equal amounts.

Celery Juice

Discard leaves, trim the base, then wash stalks and put them through the extractor. Add a few drops of lemon juice and then chill.

Cucumber Juice

Cut washed, unpeeled cucumber into strips and put through extractor. Mix with equal amount of grapefruit juice.

These are some of my favourite vegetable-juice mixes:

Zone Therapy Cocktail 1

Cut up equal amounts of celery, parsley and carrots, then put them through the juice extractor. Add a few drops of lemon or orange juice.

Zone Therapy Cocktail 2

Cut up equal amounts of apples, carrots and celery; blend, then chill before serving.

Zone Therapy Cocktail 3

Put equal amounts of chopped rhubarb and strawberries through the extractor, then flavour with honey according to taste.

Zone Therapy Cocktail 4

Put equal amounts of parsley, turnip tops, chopped celery and carrots, plus a few drops of lemon juice, through the juice extractor.

Zone Therapy Cocktail 5

Put equal amounts of chopped green peppers and celery through the extractor, adding a few drops of lemon juice.

Vitamin Supplements

Take a daily supply of vitamin D in the form of cod-liver oil capsules. An adult needs 1000 units of vitamin D daily.

The B vitamins are also vital for protecting your health. Buy these in the form of powdered brewer's yeast. Take a tablespoonful stirred into water or tomato juice three times a day before meals – you will be amazed at the pep this gives you.

Take 1000 units of vitamin C daily – this is essential for good health.

5   We have already seen how important it is to drink water when we conclude any session of Zone Therapy massage. Water helps wash away the toxins that the massage has dislodged. But I also want you to get into the habit of drinking water frequently throughout the day. Not only does the water act to sweep debris out of the system, it is also itself a vitalizing element. I suggest you drink six to eight glasses of pure water a day, ideally neither during meals nor within half an hour before or after a meal. Drink your first glass of (preferably warm) water as soon as you arise. Don't gulp it down; rather, sip slowly.

THE ZONE THERAPY 7-DAY DIET

You are now ready to start the Zone Therapy 7-Day Diet. Remember, as well as enabling you to control your weight it will build up your general health. You will feel better than you have ever felt in your life, and you can attain the shape you desire. The opportunity is yours.

Notice that one of the principles of this diet is that you should eat and/or drink small amounts on several occasions during the day rather than pigging out at just three mealtimes. In this way you give your glands the greatest help possible in converting food and drink into energy. Nevertheless, since these are all extremely healthy foods, unless a particular amount is stipulated you may eat as much as you like of the specified foods.

DAY 1

on arising: 1 glass of pure water

before breakfast: 1 tablespoon of brewer's yeast mixed into water or tomato juice

breakfast: 1 glass of fruit or vegetable juice; 1 poached egg or 2 hardboiled eggs with the yolks removed; 1 slice of brown or rye bread (toasted if you wish); black coffee

after breakfast: vitamin supplements – see page 61 for advice on quantities

midday: 1 glass of pure water

before lunch: 1 tablespoon of brewer's yeast mixed into water or tomato juice

lunch: 2 tablespoons of cottage cheese with salad of radishes, green peppers, tomatoes, celery, carrots; 1 small yoghurt

mid-afternoon: 1 small yoghurt with cinnamon to taste plus 1 teaspoon of black syrup molasses

late afternoon: 1 glass of pure water

before dinner: 1 tablespoon of brewer's yeast mixed into water or tomato juice

dinner: vegetable-juice cocktail; ½ lb broiled fat-free steak with green lightly cooked (still crisp) vegetables and mixed green salad with 1 tablespoon of French dressing

late evening: 2 glasses of pure water

before retiring: 1 small yoghurt; 1 tablespoon of brewer's yeast mixed into water or tomato juice

DAY 2

on arising: 1 glass of pure water

before breakfast: 1 tablespoon of brewer's yeast mixed into water or tomato juice

breakfast: 1 scrambled egg; 1 slice wholemeal bread (toasted if you wish); black coffee

after breakfast: vitamin supplements – see page 61 for advice on quantities

midday: 1 glass of pure water

before lunch: 1 tablespoon of brewer's yeast mixed into water or tomato juice

lunch: 2 hardboiled eggs with mixed vegetable salad; 1 yoghurt

mid-afternoon: 1 small yoghurt with cinnamon to taste plus 1 teaspoon of black syrup molasses

late afternoon: 1 glass of pure water

before dinner: 1 tablespoon of brewer's yeast mixed into water or tomato juice

dinner: 1 large glass of mixed fruit juice; broiled chicken breast with lightly cooked (still crisp) cabbage and broccoli; raw carrots and radishes with apple sauce

late evening: 2 glasses of pure water

before retiring: 1 small yoghurt with a pinch of nutmeg; 1 tablespoon of brewer's yeast mixed into water or tomato juice

DAY 3

on arising: 1 glass of pure water

before breakfast: 1 tablespoon of brewer's yeast mixed into water or tomato juice *breakfast:* 1 medium grapefruit; 3 slices of grilled crisp bacon; 1 slice of wholemeal bread or toast; black coffee

after breakfast: vitamin supplements – see page 61 for advice on quantities

midday: 1 glass of pure water

before lunch: 1 tablespoon of brewer's yeast mixed into water or tomato juice

lunch: 2 hardboiled eggs, with the yolks removed, and mixed vegetable salad; 1 yoghurt with a pinch of either nutmeg or cinnamon

mid-afternoon: 1 small yoghurt with cinnamon to taste plus 1 teaspoon of black syrup molasses

late afternoon: 1 glass of pure water

before dinner: 1 tablespoon of brewer's yeast mixed into water or tomato juice

dinner: 1 vegetable-juice cocktail; 2 grilled lamb chops with lightly cooked spinach and raw celery sticks; portion of fresh or stewed fruit

late evening: 2 glasses of pure water

before retiring: 1 small yoghurt; 1 glass of warm milk with 1 tablespoon of black syrup molasses mixed in

DAY 4

on arising: 1 glass of pure water

before breakfast: 1 tablespoon of brewer's yeast mixed into water or tomato juice

breakfast: segments of an orange soaked in fruit juice; 2 soya-bean cakes (available in health food stores); black coffee

after breakfast: vitamin supplements – see page 61 for advice on quantities

midday: 1 glass of pure water

before lunch: 1 tablespoon of brewer's yeast mixed into water or tomato juice *lunch:* 2 tablespoons of cottage cheese served with mixed vegetable salad; 1 yoghurt with a pinch of nutmeg

mid-afternoon: 1 small yoghurt with cinnamon to taste plus 1 teaspoon of black syrup molasses

late afternoon: 1 glass of pure water

before dinner: 1 tablespoon of brewer's yeast mixed into water or tomato juice

dinner: celery-and-tomato-juice cocktail; ½ lb lean steak with parsley, young onions, carrots, string beans

late evening: 2 glasses of pure water

before retiring: 1 yoghurt; 1 tablespoon of brewer's yeast mixed into water or tomato juice

DAY 5

on arising: 1 glass of pure water

before breakfast: 1 tablespoon of brewer's yeast mixed into water or tomato juice

breakfast: 1 grapefruit; 1 boiled egg; 1 slice of wholemeal or rye bread; black coffee

after breakfast: vitamin supplements – see page 61 for advice on quantities

midday: 1 glass of pure water

before lunch: 1 tablespoon of brewer's yeast mixed into water or tomato juice

lunch: 2 soya-bean cakes with vegetable salad; 1 yoghurt

mid-afternoon: 1 small yoghurt with cinnamon to taste plus 1 teaspoon of black syrup molasses

late afternoon: 1 glass of pure water

before dinner: 1 tablespoon of brewer's yeast mixed into water or tomato juice

dinner: steamed fish (any variety) with carrot soufflé, stewed tomatoes and mixed green salad with French dressing

late evening: 2 glasses of pure water

before retiring: 1 yoghurt; 1 tablespoon of brewer's yeast mixed into water or tomato juice

DAY 6

on arising: 1 glass of pure water

before breakfast: 1 tablespoon of brewer's yeast mixed into water or tomato juice

breakfast: 1 large tomato juice; 1 poached egg; 1 slice of wholemeal bread/toast; black coffee

after breakfast: vitamin supplements – see page 61 for advice on quantities

midday: 1 glass of pure water

before lunch: 1 tablespoon of brewer's yeast mixed into water or tomato juice

lunch: 2 soya-bean cakes with mixed salad of celery, parsley and sliced tomatoes; 1 yoghurt

mid-afternoon: 1 small yoghurt with cinnamon to taste plus 1 teaspoon of black syrup molasses

late afternoon: 1 glass of pure water

before dinner: 1 tablespoon of brewer's yeast mixed into water or tomato juice

dinner: grilled calves' liver and onions with lightly cooked spinach; slices of melon soaked in fruit juice

late evening: 2 glasses of pure water

before retiring: 1 yoghurt with 1 teaspoon of black syrup molasses; 1 tablespoon of brewer's yeast mixed into water or tomato juice

DAY 7

on arising: 1 glass of pure water

before breakfast: 1 tablespoon of brewer's yeast mixed into water or tomato juice

breakfast: 1 scrambled egg; 1 slice of wholemeal bread/toast; black coffee

after breakfast: vitamin supplements – see page 61 for advice on quantities

midday: 1 glass of pure water

before lunch: 1 tablespoon of brewer's yeast mixed into water or tomato juice

lunch: 2 tablespoons of cottage cheese served with tomato salad and green-vegetable salad, including green peppers; 1 yoghurt

mid-afternoon: 1 small yoghurt with cinnamon to taste plus 1 teaspoon of black syrup molasses

late afternoon: 1 glass of pure water

before dinner: 1 tablespoon of brewer's yeast mixed into water or tomato juice

dinner: vegetable soup; soya beans and mushrooms lightly sautéed, with lightly cooked spinach; stewed fruit with wheatgerm cakes (available in health food stores)

late evening: 2 glasses of pure water

before retiring: 1 yoghurt with 1 teaspoon of black syrup molasses; 1 tablespoon of brewer's yeast mixed into water or tomato juice

4

THE ZONE THERAPY LIFESTYLE

When you get to grips with your new diet and you practise the ten-minutes-a-day programme of facial exercise and massage, you will begin to feel different about yourself. You will care for yourself more. You will want to work towards your perfect self. Therefore, in addition to the two programmes I have described in the previous chapters, I am now going to give you some general advice on the Zone Therapy lifestyle – guidelines on relaxation, skin, hair and dental care and posture – which will complement the programmes, together with some simple hand, foot and tongue workouts from which you will feel great benefit, and which you will be able to practise on yourself while, for example, watching television or sitting on a train or plane.

RELAXATION

If you want a beautiful, healthy body you must make certain that you get plenty of sleep and relaxation. Your muscles need time to recuperate and to build up. If you are working during the day, particularly if you are doing a physical job, then you must remember that your muscle cells are being broken down by the repeated tension. These cells must be given rest periods to enable them to rebuild. Try to conserve your energy. Rest at all opportunities, especially after meals. Make certain that you always have at least eight hours' sleep every night.

When the mind and the body are persistently overworked through the stress and strain of our so-called civilized world which includes eating, drinking, social activities and all the other forms of entertainment available, their natural functions rapidly decrease.

Everything you do in this life requires energy. Some people spend their entire lives in a constantly tensed-up state. If you become annoyed or very angry, you will have noticed how weak you feel after the rage or anger has subsided. And in actual fact you are more tired at that moment than you would have been had you done a hard day's physical labour, because during your anger all your muscles are tensed up, your breathing becomes irregular, your eyes become wild, and all parts of your body are in a state of tension. Your heart is beating faster, your blood pressure is increased, and all this causes devastation to the digestive system. The devastation that is taking place in the nervous system is terrific.

Anxiety and worry can also cause skin troubles. Indeed, worry creates lines in your skin which age your appearance very quickly. So if you want to keep a young-looking face, then relaxation is what you must practise.

Remember that each day your body builds up the energy which is necessary for the next day and all that energy can be consumed in a few moments by bad moods, irritation, worry and anger. If you learn to relax properly you will undoubtedly build up endurance and strength. You will become vigorous and full of vitality. Take a good look at a cat. Notice how it lies down and stretches and relaxes. Notice its beautiful motion when it walks. A cat will use only the necessary amount of energy required in any situation. Most of its time is spent in a relaxed condition, but when it needs all its reflexes and energies it can summon them up in a split second and all that latent energy comes into use as it springs into action. A cat is able to do this because it knows the power of relaxation.

HOW TO RELAX

First lie down, then allow thought forms to appear and suggest to each part of your body – your feet, ankles, calves, knees, thighs, spine and the rest of your body – that it should relax. Start with your feet and work up through the legs, through the body into the head, shoulders, arms and spine. Every part of you, even your mouth, throat, tongue and eyes, should be completely relaxed. Send thought forms saying: ankle, I want you to relax; wrist, I want you to relax. Suggest to each set of muscles that they relax completely. Your fingers, toes, neck, spine; send the thought to each one.

Telling the body to relax completely is known as auto-suggestion. You are telling your muscles and your internal organs that they should relax, and they will do this if you ask them to do so in a relaxed way. Think also about your heart, kidneys, lungs and brain. They need to be able to relax and if you tell them to relax, they will do so.

Next, relax yourself mentally. You do this by concentrating purely on the breath. You breathe in and consciously send the breath to every part of your body. Breathe in slowly and just concentrate completely on breathing. It will give you a feeling of being as light as a feather and it will bring about a beautiful feeling of blissfulness, peace and joy.

Practise breathing through your nose, keeping your mouth shut. Breathe in through your nose, hold it for a few seconds and breathe out again through your nose. Let the filters in your nose take all or most of the poisons out of the air you are breathing, for the air you breathe today is full of poisons.

Every time you breathe you should exercise your stomach. If you don't, you are not breathing properly; each breath should make the stomach expand and contract.

You are totally dependent on your NERVES for if your nerves are severely overtaxed, then the weakest organ in your body will break down, being followed by the next weakest organ and so on, causing a chain reaction of break-downs.

If you have had a hard day and feel really washed out, get your partner to place one hand firmly on your forehead and one hand on your neck for a period of five minutes. You will be really amazed to find how much better you feel. Wife can do the same for husband, girlfriend for boyfriend and boyfriend for girlfriend.

Every night, brush over all the parts of your body, including legs and arms, with a hair brush. This alone will make you feel wonderful. Then into bed.

SKIN, HAIR AND DENTAL CARE

If you have blackheads or open pores, a good thing to do is to steam your face. Take a bowl and fill it with very hot water (add any kind of herb, if you wish); place the bowl on the table and cover your head with a big bath towel so that all the steam is under the towel and none of it escapes. The steam should rise straight up into your face. You will find that it penetrates deeply into your pores, so that perspiration will pour down from the open pores, loosening the accumulated dirt and rancid oils. Then, to close the pores, splash your face with cold water. Do this on three consecutive days for no more than five or ten minutes at a time. After that, one weekly treatment will help to keep all the pores clean, giving you a lovely beautiful look.

Your skin, believe it or not, does need exposure to clean fresh air – I recommend a good walk over fields or through woodlands. Air bathing, you could call it. It has enormous benefits.

Smoking is a quick way to ruin the skin. You see heavy smokers whose skin looks parched and is a yellowish colour. Nicotine plays havoc with the skin. Think of the amount of poison in tobacco smoke which you inhale and which passes down into your body through your bloodstream. If you are putting poison into your blood, how do you expect to look beautiful? If you are a heavy smoker it is impossible to have a truly healthy glowing skin.

What about your hair? If you are losing your hair, it's very worrying, isn't it? But there are things that can be done to help this condition. Rubbing your fingernails together will stimulate all the nerve endings up to the hair roots. You should buff your fingernails together for fifteen minutes a day. You don't have to do the fifteen minutes all at once – just do a few minutes at a time to make up fifteen minutes a day.

Use plenty of finger massage on the hair. Apply the fingers to the scalp and then, without lifting them, massage deep into your scalp from the back to the front until you have covered the entire head. Try to make a daily habit of giving your scalp a massage. The action induces a free flow of blood to the roots of the hair and is one more positive step towards making sure that you are doing the best you can towards keeping a beautiful head of hair.

Brush your hair regularly, taking all the dead hair out of your head. Regular brushing will remove dead roots which otherwise remain and clog the pores.

Once a week you should make a habit of gently pulling your hair. Grab hold of the tufts of hair all over the head and pull gently. As your hair strengthens you can add more strength to the tugging movement.

If you live in a city where the air is polluted your hair will need much more care than if you live in the country where the air is cleaner. Dirt blocks up the hair follicles and causes premature baldness. If you want thick hair all your life you must pay particular attention to keeping your head clean. You must see that it gets plenty of air and sunshine. Never wear a tight hat because this blocks off the air supply and induces sweat which corrodes the hair. Keep your combs and brushes scrupulously clean. Be careful what you use in the form of hair sprays and lacquers because they settle, crystallize and eat into the pores, clogging them up.

The sun is vital for good hair because the energy it gives to the hair strengthens it and encourages growth. Try to let the sun reach the roots of your hair as much as possible. Walk out in the wind, let the wind flow through your hair. This is immensely invigorating, stimulating and exhilarating.

Your hair is made of protein so you must make certain that you are getting adequate supplies of good protein. Fish, nuts, cheese, milk, poultry, plus a small quantity of meat, soya beans and eggs, will provide the protein which is essential for good health.

Always see your dentist regularly. Make sure that your teeth are in first-class condition. Bad teeth poison the bloodstream, and can be the cause of many diseases. If you have bad teeth then that condition, for instance, indirectly helps to poison your scalp. Try if possible always to clean your mouth and your teeth after each and every meal.

CORRECT POSTURE

The majority of people hold their bodies incorrectly, allowing the abdomen to swell out. Incorrect breathing causes the abdomen to enlarge, resulting in a sagging of the colons, internal organs and intestines. This is what I call a 'corporation', a swollen stomach. This incorrect breathing and the sagging of the abdomen muscles pulls forward on the lumbar and the dorsal areas of the spine. Not only is this unattractive but it will, if allowed to continue, cause the arches to fall; you will lose control over all the back muscles and the muscles in the stomach will begin to dissipate.

So learn to walk and sit straight. Walk erectly. Breathe deeply and steadily and consciously hold the abdomen up by the internal muscles. You must walk with shoulders back, head erect and abdomen up and in. You should breathe deeply, pull your abdomen in and lift your chest up. You must practise this to regain control over your abdominal muscles. Your organs will drop by as much as four inches if ignored. Draw in your lower stomach muscles as low down in the abdomen as possible and lift up and in as strongly a you are able. Think that your lower stomach is being lifted up almost to your chest and throat; that is the feeling you should aim for. Practise it all the time when you are running, walking, sitting, or lying on your back. If you do this over a period of a couple of months, you will train and rebuild your stomach muscles. In the beginning you will feel discomfort because the muscles will not want to work, but you must persist to regain correct posture. The reward is well worth the trouble. You will find that your fallen arches will straighten up and your height will increase. In addition, your bowel action and your digestion and general health will benefit.

Asthma and bronchial lung diseases and awful diseases of the stomach can be related to organs being in a prolapsed condition. Get your stomach in and up. Walk as if you are ten feet tall. Practise and practise until the exercise is second nature.

GENERAL EXERCISES FOR THE TONGUE, THE FEET AND THE HANDS

As well as on the surface of the face, the nerve endings of the ten zones also meet on the tongue, the feet and the hands. Working on the face as described in Chapter 2 has the special advantage of benefiting directly the muscles and skin of the most important part of our bodies for presenting ourselves to the world. In terms of internal health and general youthfulness, though, the tongue, the feet and the hands are just as important as the face. In fact because we can generally bear greater pressure on these areas, particularly on the points of the feet, these other parts of the body are often more important for treating particular ailments, as we shall see in Chapter 5. Now, though, I want to introduce you to the pressure points of the tongue, the feet and the hands and to teach you some general exercises you can practise on these areas, all of which will help you on the road to youthfulness, beauty and health.

THE TONGUE

The tongue is unique because all ten zones meet there in such a small area. So exercising the tongue is a quick and easy way to tone up your entire body.

THE FEET

Particularly in the case of the feet, many people find it easier and more pleasant to work with a partner, though if you are supple it is perfectly possible to work on yourself.

When applying treatment use the inward, medial side of the thumb or the first finger. Keep the nails well trimmed.

Exercise one

Massage the tongue by taking the handle of a dessert spoon and putting pressure on the tongue. Press each area for ten seconds then move onto the next one. Where there is a painful area, it means there is congestion and it should be worked out. Press the tongue all over for a period of two minutes.

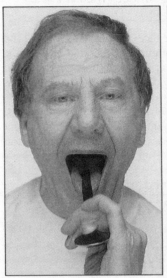
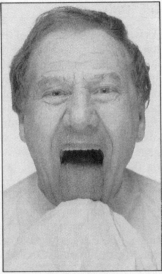

Exercise two

Take hold of your tongue with a dry piece of cloth, perhaps a handkerchief or a towel, and pull it gently as you move it about. This exercises the sixty-odd muscles in your throat, and a session of just one minute will help tone up your entire system.

Exercise three

It is tremendously beneficial to scrub the tongue clean with a toothbrush every morning before breakfast, and also to perform the same simple massage before going to sleep. This will help rid your whole body of toxins.

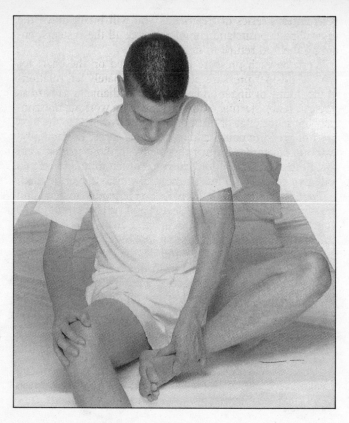

Take the foot and hold it firmly with one hand. Then place the thumb or finger of the other hand onto the area you are going to work upon and apply firm pressure with a rotating movement.

I repeat: some people can take more pressure than others. You will find your own level by what you feel. After a while you will be able to massage more deeply as you remove the condition. Where there is deep congestion it will be tender, so use your common sense and don't work at it too vigorously. Give painful areas a few seconds' pressure, then move on and come back to the tender places after a short rest. After a series of treatments you will break down the crystalline deposits and completely free all the systems, enabling them to return to normal activity.

Work on each pressure point indicated on the chart for ten seconds per pressure point (approximately ten rotations of the thumb or finger on half an inch in diameter as hard as you can bear), starting on the big toe, then working horizontally out to the edge of the foot; move downwards to the next layer of pressure points and again move across horizontally, working outwards. Return repeatedly to those tender areas that need special attention for a total of ten minutes and you will give yourself the most beneficial workout ever devised.

To those people on their own who are unable to bend and are unable to work their own feet, a golf ball is helpful. Take your shoes and socks off and sit on a chair. Place the golf ball on the floor and roll the right foot over the ball for a few minutes. Then change over and do the same with the left foot. Great benefit can come from this form of treatment.

If you can, try to prevent corns, bunions, etc., growing on the foot, as these often sit over the top of a pressure point and make it impossible to work.

THE HANDS

Massage of the hands has the added advantage of being inconspicuous, so that, if you feel like it, you can give yourself a thorough Zone Therapy workout in public without causing alarm!

In the case of the hands it is possible to have a partner massage them for you, but more people prefer to work on themselves. When you are treating the hands, use the thumb of one hand to treat the other hand. Start massaging the hand at the tip of the thumb and work with pressure all over it, including the sides and also the back. Work down and into the webbing part of the thumb too. Be systematic about it and leave out none of the pressure points in the chart; as with the feet, work for ten seconds on each point, returning repeatedly to sore spots. Then do the same with the fingers. Work over each finger from the tip, applying pressure to the underneath, the sides and the back and down into the webbing of each finger. Remember that if you apply pressure over the top joints of your thumbs and fingers it will give the entire body a good toning-up. As with the feet, always start on the inner edge of the hand and work horizontally towards the outer edge, massaging each joint and pressure point in turn; having completed one level, go down to the next one.

Finally, rub one set of fingernails vigorously against the other for a minute to complete the treatment.

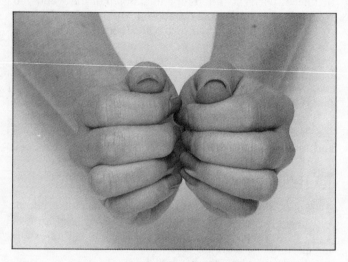

Another very beneficial exercise with the hands, which I often practise while I am watching television, is to wrap elastic bands round the tips of the fingers and thumb of one hand. You must put them on tightly until the tips of your fingers turn blue. Try to keep them on for a minute, then put them on the other hand. Because each of the ten zones is connected to an individual finger, your whole body will feel the benefit immediately. An alternative is to put a wooden clothes peg on each finger and thumb. Put them first over the nails, then over the sides. Try to keep them on for five minutes on each hand.

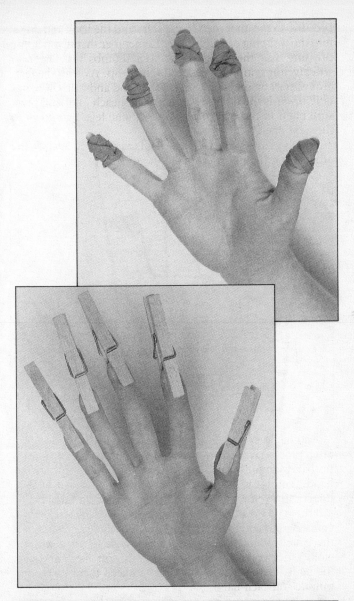

Pressure points – the hands

As with the feet, always start on the inner edge of the hand and work horizontally towards the outer edge, massaging each joint and pressure point in turn; having completed one level, go down to the next one.

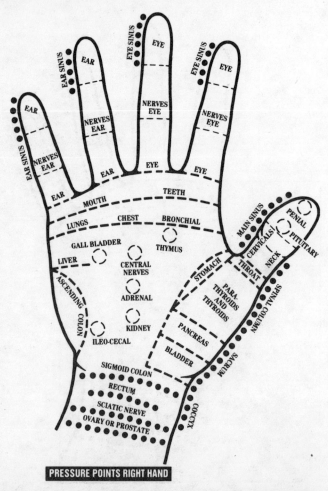

PRESSURE POINTS RIGHT HAND

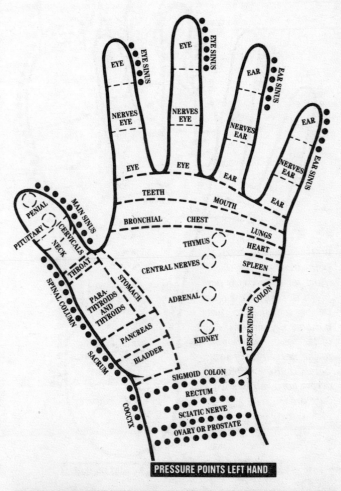

PRESSURE POINTS LEFT HAND

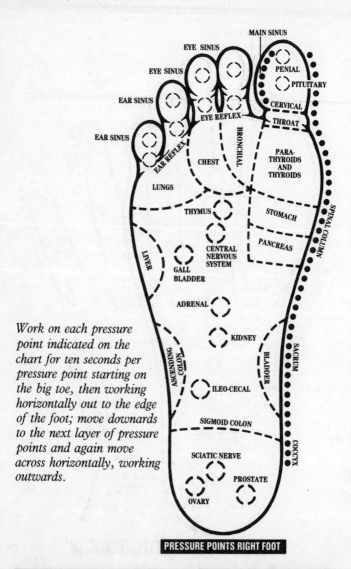

Work on each pressure
point indicated on the
chart for ten seconds per
pressure point starting on
the big toe, then working
horizontally out to the edge
of the foot; move downwards
to the next layer of pressure
points and again move
across horizontally, working
outwards.

MAIN SINUS
EYE SINUS
EYE SINUS
PENIAL
EAR SINUS
PITUITARY
CERVICAL
EAR SINUS
EYE REFLEX
THROAT
EAR REFLEX
BRONCHIAL
PARA-
THYROIDS
AND
THYROIDS
CHEST
LUNGS
SPINAL COLUMN
THYMUS
STOMACH
CENTRAL
NERVOUS
SYSTEM
PANCREAS
LIVER
GALL
BLADDER
ADRENAL
KIDNEY
ASCENDING COLON
BLADDER
SACRUM
ILEO-CECAL
SIGMOID COLON
COCCYX
SCIATIC NERVE
PROSTATE
OVARY

PRESSURE POINTS RIGHT FOOT

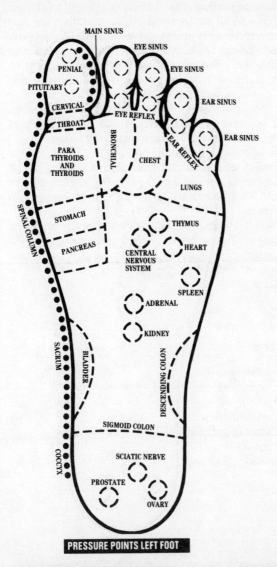

PRESSURE POINTS LEFT FOOT

You will find that pressure over the fingers and the toes alone will help to prevent many conditions. Daily work over all the fingers and all the toes will help to stimulate the nervous systems and builds up the nerve strength in the body. It will help to relieve many symptoms: it will ease nausea or any form of travel sickness; it is good for neuralgia, neuritis or cramps; it helps to stimulate the circulation (use this treatment if you suffer from cold feet or cold hands). You can take a nice, mild wire brush and stroke over your feet, hands and up your arms. Always stroke upwards, never downwards. This helps to stimulate the circulation.

All kinds of complaints will respond to this form of treatment – stomach aches, fatigue, ulcerated stomachs, throat troubles, laryngitis, loss of voice, indigestion, even pain in your mouth from bad teeth or gums, will all respond to zonal treatments.

Throughout all your Zone Therapy exercises, whether on the face, tongue, feet or hands, keep a mental image of the youthful, beautiful healthy you that you are striving to construct. Say to yourself, 'I will succeed', and your life will be a daily miracle.

5

ZONE THERAPY'S A-Z OF CURES

FOR SPECIAL PROBLEMS

During thirty years of practising Zone Therapy I have found that most illnesses will respond to it and that often miraculous results are obtained. Every family can benefit from these treatments.

The ideal situation, of course, is to have the good sense to apply this form of treatment whilst you are still healthy. If we all did that, 95 per cent of us would never be sick. But no. We wait until we are nearly dead before we decide to do anything about our condition. So, my advice is this. Once you are back to normal health use Zone Therapy for the rest of your days and remain healthy. Be determined never to be sick again.

REMEMBER

You may find Zone Therapy is quite painful in the beginning but, over a period of time, as you eliminate poison from the particular nerve ending and stimulate the gland, the painful areas will decrease, until eventually there is no tenderness left in that particular area. And although it is sometimes painful, you can use Zone Therapy safely. It cannot harm you. Those who are sick, begin now, and discover the way back to good health, which is surely your first big step towards true happiness. Your rate of success in curing an illness, of course, depends on how deep-seated your condition is.

DRINK WATER

Always drink a glass of water after each treatment. This helps to flush toxins out of the body. When you apply pressure to areas such as the feet, hands and ears, you are breaking down crystalline deposits that are choking the life out of those nerve endings. A glass of water will help the body rid itself of any unwanted matter.

ANAEMIA

For those who suffer from anaemia, the spleen is of paramount importance as it is here that iron is stored, and it is lack of iron in the blood which causes anaemia. This can cause serious problems if not diagnosed and attended to. Women are more prone to anaemia than men because they require more iron. So, if you discover any tenderness in the area of the foot where treatment for the spleen is applied, you are probably anaemic. Happily, improvement is rapid unless you suffer from pernicious anaemia and then, of course, improvement will be slower.

The spleen lies under the heart, which is to the left side of the body. The spleen is a gland whose size and weight is liable to variation at different periods of life. On average, it is about five inches long and is about seven ounces in weight.

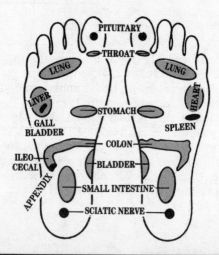

This gland has a great effect upon the intestines so work should be undertaken upon the colon, liver, adrenals, pituitary and thyroid, as well as the spleen. Use your thumb in a rotating movement directly over the sore spot. A course of

SPLEEN REFLEXES

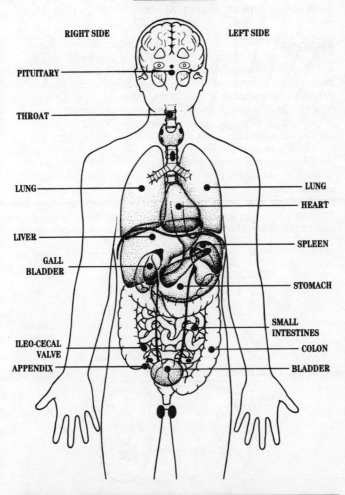

RIGHT SIDE

LEFT SIDE

PITUITARY

THROAT

LUNG

LIVER

GALL BLADDER

ILEO-CECAL VALVE

APPENDIX

LUNG

HEART

SPLEEN

STOMACH

SMALL INTESTINES

COLON

BLADDER

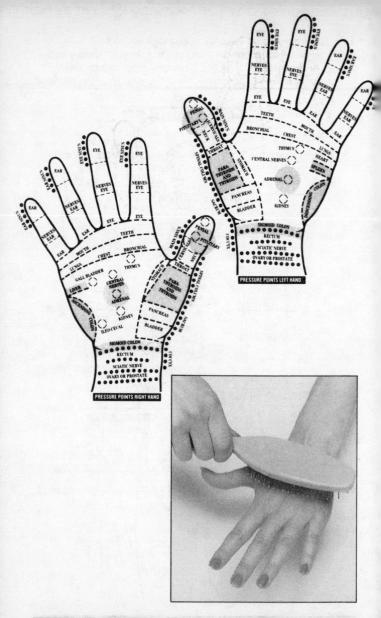

PRESSURE POINTS RIGHT HAND

PRESSURE POINTS LEFT HAND

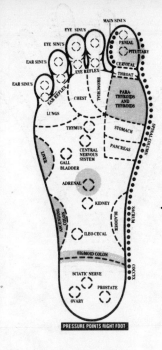

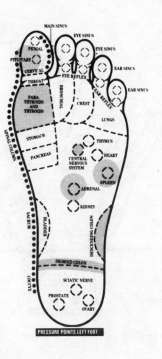

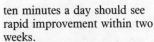

ten minutes a day should see rapid improvement within two weeks.

Stroke your body with a brush night and morning, all over if possible, and especially from the fingertips up to the shoulders. Use swift light strokes upwards towards the heart. This is great for the circulation and will give you extra get-up-and-go.

Eat plenty of lettuce and food with a high mineral content such as grilled lean meat and liver. And make sure you have plenty of vitamin C.

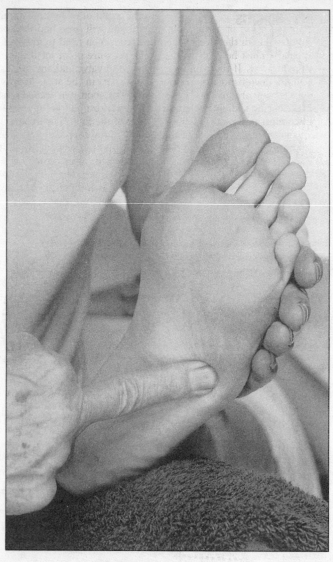

Massaging the descending colon

APPENDICITIS

Any trouble in the area of the appendix must be dealt with straight away. If the pain is acute, a doctor must be seen at once. If you are just experiencing a slight twinge or discomfort in the area of the appendix, in the middle of the stomach on the right-hand side, Zone Therapy can help you. Pressure with your thumb will tell if there is congestion or not around the appendix.

The appendix point on the foot is rather small so if you are unable to put enough strength behind your thumb pressure use the rounded end of a pencil or something similar and you will soon find the spot exactly. You need to massage the pressure point for the ileocecal valve and any other sore spots in the area. Massage only for about ten seconds then give it a rest and go to another part of the foot. Then come back to the sore spot and give it another ten seconds. Give it a rest then, again, come back and try fifteen seconds. Keep doing this until all the soreness has gone.

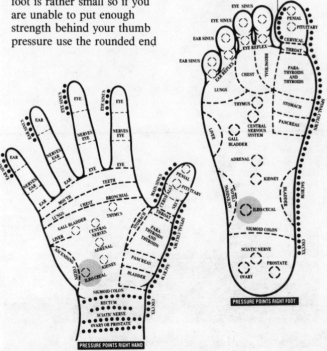

PRESSURE POINTS RIGHT HAND

PRESSURE POINTS RIGHT FOOT

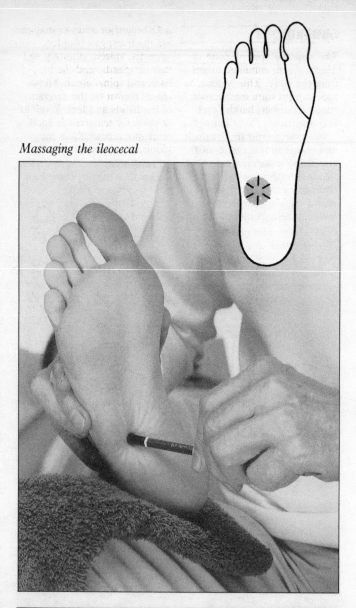

Massaging the ileocecal

ARTHRITIS

The main purpose of Zone Therapy is to eliminate toxins from the body. This is done by applying pressure over certain parts of the feet, hands, ears and tongue.

In cases of arthritis, I usually find that the most congested area is the kidneys. Remember that your arthritic condition is there as a result of too much acidity building up in your body, and the kidneys have to get rid of it. So, work gently but firmly over the kidney areas as shown on the diagrams.

Other major areas to massage are the liver, gall bladder, adrenals, spleen, pituitary and thyroid glands, and the hip, back and spinal areas. These are all shown on the diagrams of the hands and feet. Work all of these for ten seconds each, returning repeatedly to the kidney for a total of ten minutes a day.

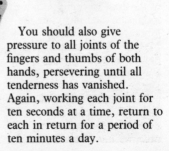

PRESSURE POINTS LEFT HAND

PRESSURE POINTS RIGHT HAND

You should also give pressure to all joints of the fingers and thumbs of both hands, persevering until all tenderness has vanished. Again, working each joint for ten seconds at a time, return to each in return for a period of ten minutes a day.

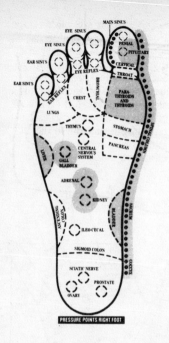
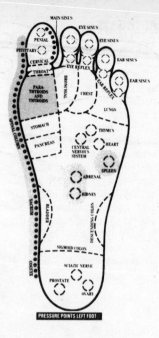

PRESSURE POINTS RIGHT FOOT

PRESSURE POINTS LEFT FOOT

The next stage is to attend to the ears. Using the first finger and thumb in a pinching action, massage the entire area of both ears and, most importantly, pay special attention to the outside edges of the ears, working from top to bottom, and including the lobes, for five minutes. Massage on the ears must be done very gently, as if you are rubbing face cream into the skin.

Then, using the handle of a large spoon, apply pressure all over the tongue, covering as much of it as you comfortably can. This should be done for two minutes each day.

Also, it is a good practice to take two teaspoonfuls of crude black syrup molasses each day in warm water, or in its raw state, depending upon your taste. Also, each day, drink a dessertspoonful of cider vinegar and a big teaspoonful of honey diluted in a cup of hot water. Take this twice a day if you can. Three times a week take a warm bath and add a cupful of Epsom Salts, bathing your affected joints for ten minutes, then straight into a warm bed with a warm drink.

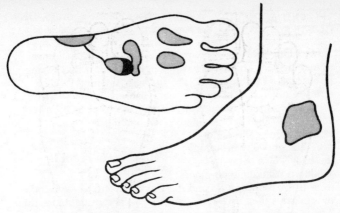

Massaging the kidney

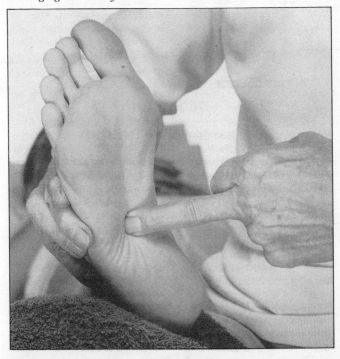

THE ANTI-ARTHRITIS CAPSULE

Now, I must tell you something very exciting. I have formulated a capsule for arthritis sufferers. The first part of the capsule contains an amino acid called DL-Phenylalanine. This is not a drug but works by protecting the body's own naturally produced painkilling hormones from being broken down and it thus extends their activity. Amino acid is nature's painkiller, helping the body to heal from within, and it also acts as an antidepressant. In most cases it is effective against the chronic pain of osteoarthritis, rheumatoid arthritis, low back pain, menstrual cramps, migraine headache, joint pains, long-standing whiplash, post-operative pain and neuralgia. It is nonaddictive and its effects are cumulative. Patients do not develop tolerance to its pain-relieving effects and there are no side-effects. It can be combined with other existing therapy drugs, aspirin and acupuncture.

People who suffer from chronic pain have lower levels of endorphin activity in their blood and cerebrospinal fluid and, since DL-Phenylalanine can restore normal endorphin levels, it can thereby assist the body in reducing pain naturally without the use of drugs. DL-Phenylalanine is capable of selective pain blocking and can effectively alleviate chronic long-term pain while leaving the body's natural defence mechanisms for short-term acute pain, such as burns or cuts, unhindered.

THE GREEN-LIPPED MUSSEL

The ingredient of the second part of the capsule comes from the green-lipped mussel which is found only in the waters around New Zealand. This mussel has been deeply researched by Dr Bob Borland who is Head of the Department of Applied Biology at the Royal Institute of Technology. Overwhelming evidence, from a four-year study, shows it contains a powerful anti-inflammatory and anti-arthritic substance; Doctor Borland's study has demonstrated that there is a powerful ingredient in the green-lipped mussel which is a safe natural alternative to drug treatments.

In an age when some drug therapies that were once fully approved have had to be removed from sale because they have side-effects, the Joseph Corvo Formula capsule must give tremendous encouragement to all arthritic sufferers, for an effective and safe treatment is now available and is not a drug but a food supplement. It has been successful in relieving different forms of arthritis in many countries around the world.

The capsule should be taken *with* meals, not between. I have personally suffered with osteoarthritis in my right knee because of an injury sustained while playing football thirty-five years ago. I developed chronic pain and warping of the right knee. Now, I have to tell you, I am totally free from any pain or discomfort and my knee feels perfectly normal and acts in a perfectly normal fashion. I can walk, run, dance and exercise once again after thinking this would never be possible. To me it's just fantastic! I take three capsules every morning with my breakfast, which makes them easy to digest. Because it is an antidepressant also, I feel brighter and more mentally alert. So taking them at breakfast provides a good start to the day.

If you suffer from high blood pressure, or any heart complaint, you must first consult your doctor before starting treatment. If you are allergic to shellfish then obviously this treatment will not be suitable for you. But the majority of arthritics could start taking it now. It is called 'The Joseph Corvo PERNAMER FORMULA'.

DOGS AND CATS

The capsules I have just described have also proven wonderful in the treatment of dogs and cats. Owners have reported that their elderly, lethargic dogs have suddenly changed into enthusiastic vibrant creatures, lively and full of bounce, meeting them with a wagging tail. Alsatians, labradors, and German shepherd dogs which were about to be put down due to age or infirmity, usually with arthritis in the back hip and leg joints, have been given a completely new lease of life after a course on this extract. It is also excellent for cats.

ASTHMA, HAY FEVER

Never breathe through the mouth. If you do, stop it. You must discipline yourself and continually practise breathing through the nose. Avoid shallow breathing into the chest; this is known as clavicular breathing and is extremely bad for you. Breathe as deep down into the stomach as possible because, otherwise, you are breathing into the upper part of the lungs when the feeling you actually want is that the whole stomach area is reacting to the breath you are taking into your body. If you cannot breathe through your nose then consult your physician and discover the reason why.

Commence treatment by applying pressure in the mouth, first of all starting on the floor of the mouth under the tongue. You can do this

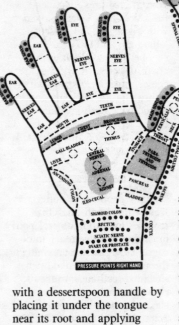

PRESSURE POINTS RIGHT HAND

PRESSURE POINTS LEFT HAND

with a dessertspoon handle by placing it under the tongue near its root and applying pressure. Hold this for two minutes, if possible, then leave it. Next day try three minutes and then keep it to a three-minute pressure each day. Next go for pressure all over the top of the tongue, applying pressure strongly over all parts of it for a period of three minutes. The tongue controls

all the zone areas of the body, and you can also help yourself by biting your tongue (not too deeply). You can certainly go over all parts of it with your teeth and it does help. Again, take hold of your tongue with a clean handkerchief, or a small towel, and pull your tongue out as far as possible and move it from side to side. Do this tongue pulling and the side-to-side movements for three minutes twice a day.

Treatment must also be given to the lungs and chest area. As the bronchial tubes are deep in the chest you may need to use a pencil or something similar. These

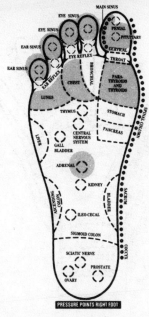

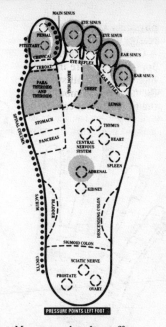

PRESSURE POINTS RIGHT FOOT

PRESSURE POINTS LEFT FOOT

pressure points are on the pads of the feet below the toes, and you must also work over the adrenal glands together with the thyroid and pituitary glands. Work upon the lungs, chest and all sinus pressure points. If you are right-handed, hold the foot with the left hand and use the right hand for the massage and vice versa if you are left-handed. Work on each point in turn for ten seconds for a total of ten minutes a day.

Rubber bands can also be worn fairly tightly around the first joints of the fingers and thumbs several times a day for one minute's duration at each session on each hand.

Many people who suffer from asthma and bronchial troubles tend to have prolapsed organs so it is necessary to do exercises in order to strengthen the diaphragm and abdomen. For instance, when you walk pull the stomach muscles in and up, hold, then release. Keep doing this exercise all the time whenever possible. If you work as instructed you will be greatly pleased with the results.

If you are determined and patient enough and are willing to work hard you can overcome almost anything, but you do need guts and staying power – so get your priorities right and go for it.

Almost everyone suffers from back problems at some time during their lifetime, even if it is only a vague pain situated somewhere in the back. Most of these problems are caused

PRESSURE POINTS LEFT HAND

PRESSURE POINTS RIGHT HAND

by a pinched nerve or muscular contraction causing congestion and, here again, Zone Therapy can and does have a wonderful effect.

The spinal column is the centre of the body, so the pressure point for it lies along the first zone of each foot from the top of the big toe down to

the bottom of the heel. The big toe corresponds to the head; follow downwards with the centre of the foot corresponding to the spine. If you follow this principle, you will have no trouble at all in locating the exact spot which you wish to manipulate along your back. For instance, if you have a pain in your lumbar region, you will follow the pressure point down towards the heel until you locate the sore spot. When you have located the area, begin your massage gently, increasing the

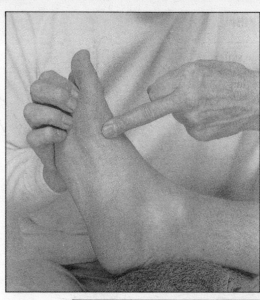

Massaging the top of the spine

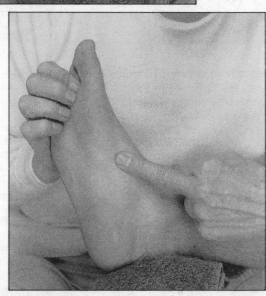

Massaging the middle of the spine

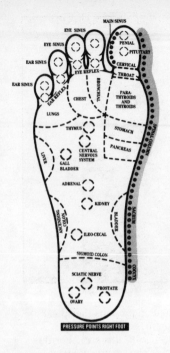

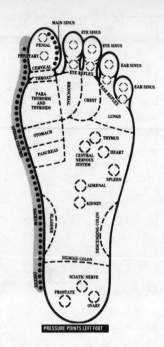

PRESSURE POINTS RIGHT FOOT

PRESSURE POINTS LEFT FOOT

pressure as you get used to it and until all the tenderness has gone. You can actually work upon your back pressure point in this way for at least twenty minutes. If, however, the pain is actually in the spine, work over all the spinal area as given on your charts with a pencil with a rounded end.

Lumbago responds very quickly to Zone Therapy and I have cured many cases with one or two treatments. One of the best therapies for lumbago is the use of an aluminium comb. The way to use the comb is to press the teeth of it against the inner surfaces of the fingers of each hand and then against the palms of the hand. For wonderful results try this for fifteen or, if you can, twenty minutes. You must also work upon the webs between the thumb and the first finger, ensuring that the fleshy part of the thumb is involved. See that the entire palm of the hand is involved in the comb treatment and you will be amazed at the results. Also use clothes pegs fastened to the tips of the fingers and thumbs. The

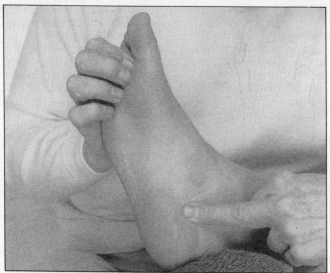

Massaging the bottom of the spine

clothes pegs should be left on for ten minutes each time you give treatment.

Massage all spinal reflexes and the hip and back areas. Also work on the kidneys and bladder area, prostrate or ovary and the colons. All this should be done on both the hands and feet, dividing the time equally. The top joints of the thumbs and all fingers must also be massaged, as must the lung, chest and bronchial areas. Work each pressure point and joint for ten seconds each, doing them in rotation for ten minutes a day.

Using the handle of a large spoon, apply pressure all over the tongue. The centre of the tongue represents the spinal column, so give special attention to this area. For this part of the treatment allow three minutes.

Massage all areas of both ears with the thumb and first finger, but particularly the lower halves, for three minutes. Work well and you will find tremendous relief from this condition. Gradually increase the pressure you give as you get better.

The treatments just described may seem simple but are tremendously effective and illustrate, yet again, that Zone Therapy brings lasting freedom from pain.

BLADDER CONDITIONS

Inflammation of the bladder is a very common condition and most of us at some time during our lives are going to have problems in this area, feeling a constant urge to urinate. Bladder conditions respond to Zone Therapy very well indeed; work is required on both feet. First, massage the bladder pressure point, then extend the treatment to the kidney pressure point because often it is the uric acid formed in the kidneys that causes inflammation of the bladder. Work both alternately for twenty-second periods for a total of ten minutes a day.

Both areas are in Zone 1 so you cannot make any mistakes. Be persistent but do not use too much pressure because, if you do have a problem in your bladder, it will be very tender when you touch the pressure point. However, at the same time work deep enough to locate the sore spots. After three of four treatments you will notice it is not so sore and, also, that you are no longer wanting to urinate every five minutes.

Use rubber bands wound around the thumb and first finger of both hands at least five times per day for periods of about ten minutes' duration each time.

PRESSURE POINTS LEFT HAND

PRESSURE POINTS RIGHT HAND

Work upon the tongue with a dessert/teaspoon handle or tooth brush handle for two minutes a day.

Drink four pints of hot water a day – as hot as you can manage.

Should there be blood in the urine and the condition persists, consult your doctor.

Massaging the bladder

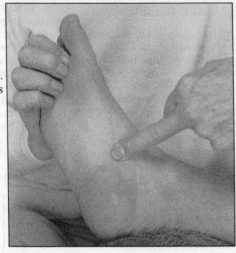

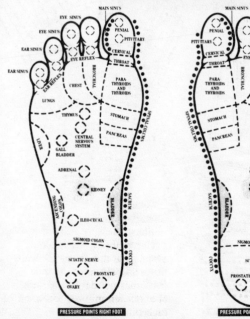

PRESSURE POINTS RIGHT FOOT

PRESSURE POINTS LEFT FOOT

HIGH BLOOD PRESSURE

Hypertension (high blood pressure) indicates a deficiency and irregularity in the functioning of the glandular system. It is the duty of the glands to supply the body with the correct amount of hormones and adrenalin to normalize the circulation which is of vital importance in maintaining proper chemical balance.

Therefore, if elimination is faulty, congestion occurs somewhere. For instance, if we have an abnormal amount of calcium, this will stick to the walls of the arteries so that they no longer retain their normal elasticity. This increases the effort put upon the heart in performing its duty.

If a person is in a highly nervous state this automatically creates imbalance in the digestion. By removing the tension and reorganizing the balance of the glandular system we can bring about a

PRESSURE POINTS LEFT HAND

wonderful change in this condition.

Blood pressure is often a problem during the latter years. It occurs when the walls of the blood vessels become smaller. As the walls become smaller, the pressure becomes greater. The danger of

PRESSURE POINTS RIGHT HAND

tremendous pressure against the walls of the blood vessels is that it may cause a blood vessel to break. When this happens a clot is formed which may lodge in the small capillaries of the brain, causing paralysis; or it could happen in the heart muscles and cause angina – such a clot can hinder the flow of blood to the heart to such an extent as to be fatal.

If a person gets into a highly nervous state, this can cause the tissues in the wall of the blood vessels to contract. During strong emotions the body normally prepares itself for the action necessary to overcome this difficulty, and the walls of the blood vessels normally contract in order to withstand the extra presure. Such blood pressure can be made normal only when the mental state which is causing it is removed. Therefore, anyone suffering from high blood pressure should always try to remain calm and relaxed at all times because sudden activity of any part of the body increases the blood pressure in that part of the body.

By carefully observing my rules, you will begin to gain

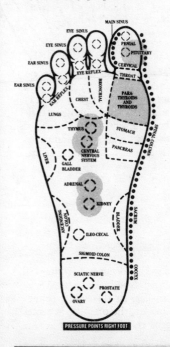

PRESSURE POINTS RIGHT FOOT

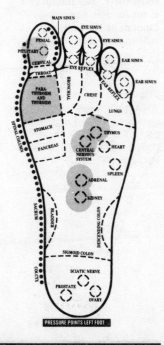

PRESSURE POINTS LEFT FOOT

control over your condition. You can see now how vital it is to keep the circulation of the body in perfect condition. You can see how vital it is that all glandular systems should be kept in perfect condition. This is your body. It is the only one you possess. Therefore, it is up to you to take particularly good care of it.

If you suffer from high blood pressure, you must see your physician at once, then you can help yourself a great deal with Zone Therapy. Your first problem is how to acquire peace of mind; the last thing you need is aggravation and upsets of any kind. Now, I cannot change your environment but, I can tell you this, by working upon your liver, kidneys, thyroid glands, adrenals, pituitary and thymus glands and nervous system, you are giving yourself the best chance of overcoming your problem. Work on these pressure points in rotation for ten seconds each for a total of ten minutes on each hand and foot.

Apply rubber bands to both thumbs and first and second fingers on the first joints, leave for one minute, then take off and allow the circulation to work through the fingers. Then put the rubber bands back on for a further one minute, repeating this several times a day.

Apply pressure to the crown of the head, down on to the neck and shoulders, up the side of the neck from the shoulders, to behind the ears. Do this for about ten minutes a day. It sounds like hard work but it is worthwhile.

LOW BLOOD PRESSURE

The treatment for low blood pressure is exactly the same as for high blood pressure. In addition, stroke and brush the body, always upwards towards the heart, for five minutes twice a day, beginning at the fingers.

CANCER OF THE BREAST AND OTHER CANCERS

Work over all glands in the body. Look at the full charts showing you where they are located and bring them up to 100 per cent fitness. Also apply pressure to the tongue, all over, from the tip of the tongue to as far back as is comfortable. Wear rubber bands over fingers and the knuckles of the fingers. Work on the pads of the feet below the toes right across the feet; also across the pads of the hands below the fingers.

Get working on the liver, pancreas, adrenals, thyroids, thymus, pituitary, kidneys and any other gland or organ as, already stated, you need all organs and glands to work at 100 per cent capacity. Spend five minutes a day on each hand and foot. This will enable you to be strong and fit. Remember, when you begin your radiotherapy and chemotherapy, that chemotherapy kills off cells. You want to be in a position to create new cells as quickly as possible, to give you a real fighting chance.

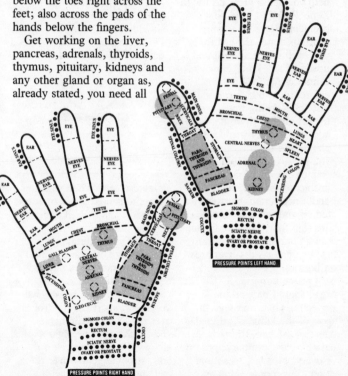

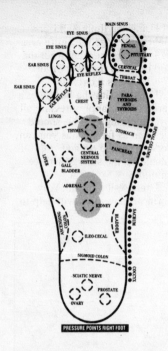
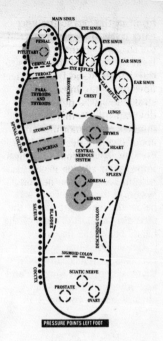

PRESSURE POINTS RIGHT FOOT

PRESSURE POINTS LEFT FOOT

CIRCULATION PROBLEMS

This is a condition where the hands and feet are constantly cold. If you feel like that it is a sure sign that your circulation is in a poor state. Work must first be done on the liver area on both the hands and feet. It is of prime importance that this organ should be working perfectly. Then, massage the areas of the kidneys, adrenals, pancreas, spleen, thyroids, parathyroids, pituitary, prostate or ovary, bladder, ascending colon, descending colon and sigmoid colon. When working upon the hands, apply pressure to the top joints of all fingers and the thumbs, paying attention to the pituitary zone in the centre of each thumb. Spend five minutes a day on each hand and foot.

With a soft wire brush give very light, short, rapid strokes over the backs of the hands and up the arms to as far as the elbows. Do the same with the legs, stroking gently over the feet and up the backs and fronts of the legs to the knees. After a few treatments, extend the stroking all the way up from the backs of the hands to the shoulders and from the feet upwards to the hips. Always stroke upwards, not downwards. Do this for two minutes in the morning and about five minutes in the evening. Apart from helping to improve circulation it will also help to build up the nervous system.

Using the thumb and first finger, massage the entire area of both ears working from the top down to the bottom for four minutes a day.

Finally, with the handle of a large spoon, apply pressure all over the tongue. This should be from as far back as you can, forward to the tip and including the sides, for three minutes.

Exercise if you can. Any form of movement will help to

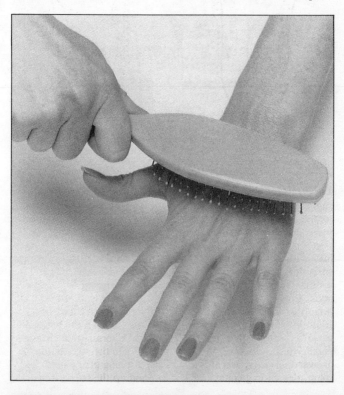

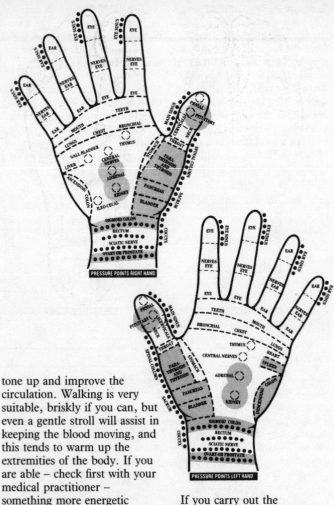

PRESSURE POINTS RIGHT HAND

PRESSURE POINTS LEFT HAND

tone up and improve the circulation. Walking is very suitable, briskly if you can, but even a gentle stroll will assist in keeping the blood moving, and this tends to warm up the extremities of the body. If you are able – check first with your medical practitioner – something more energetic would be of benefit. If you are not able to walk, then any movement of your arms, legs or body that you can manage is better than none.

If you carry out the treatment given here, you will soon see a remarkable change in your circulation. All you have to do is to be patient and determined.

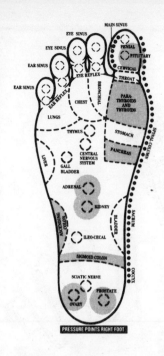

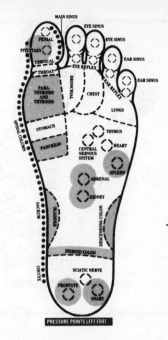

PRESSURE POINTS RIGHT FOOT

PRESSURE POINTS LEFT FOOT

COLDS

What a bore the common cold is! Without a doubt, it is the most irritating and inconvenient indisposition one can think of. Millions are spent on so-called cures and what happens is a great big nothing; you just have to live through it and wait for the next one.

By keeping every gland in the best working order and taking a good daily dose of vitamin C, it is possible to avoid catching colds altogether. So, look at the full charts of the feet and work upon every gland and organ on each foot. If you do catch a cold in the meantime, work on all glands and organs and be sure to work particularly over all the areas marked sinus – the big toe sinuses and all the other toe sinuses.

Pay particular attention, too, to the lungs and the kidneys. Having a cold means congestion, so when you work over the sinuses you will find a lot of tenderness and soreness.

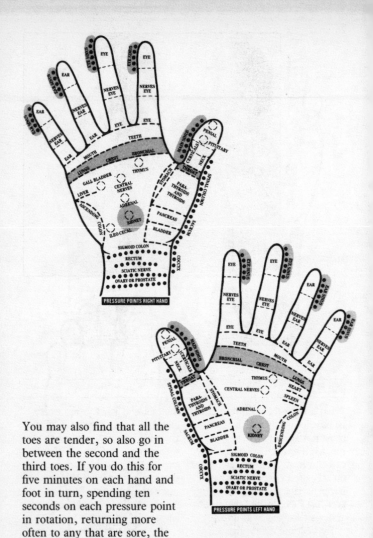

PRESSURE POINTS RIGHT HAND

PRESSURE POINTS LEFT HAND

You may also find that all the toes are tender, so also go in between the second and the third toes. If you do this for five minutes on each hand and foot in turn, spending ten seconds on each pressure point in rotation, returning more often to any that are sore, the relief that you will experience is fantastic.

Get into a warm bed as soon as possible. Drink four pints of hot water a day – as hot as possible – and eat very little; drink hot drinks frequently and keep very warm. Two days of this treatment and you will be mostly over your cold.

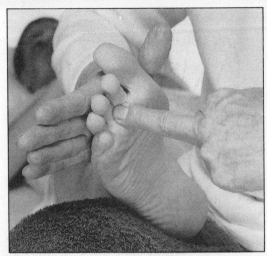

*Massaging
the chest*

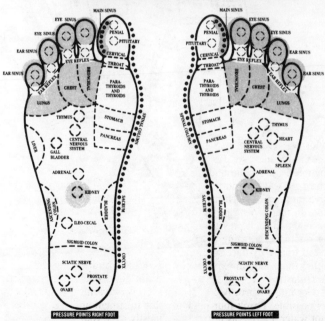

PRESSURE POINTS RIGHT FOOT

Right foot labels:
MAIN SINUS
EYE SINUS
EYE SINUS
EAR SINUS
EAR SINUS
EAR REFLEX
LUNGS
THYMUS
LIVER
GALL BLADDER
ADRENAL
KIDNEY
ASCENDING COLON
ILEO-CECAL
SIGMOID COLON
SCIATIC NERVE
OVARY
PROSTATE
PENIAL
PITUITARY
CERVICAL
THROAT
BRONCHIAL
CHEST
EYE REFLEX
PARA-THYROIDS AND THYROIDS
STOMACH
PANCREAS
CENTRAL NERVOUS SYSTEM
BLADDER
SACRUM
COCCYX
VERTEBRAE

PRESSURE POINTS LEFT FOOT

Left foot labels:
MAIN SINUS
PENIAL
PITUITARY
CERVICAL
THROAT
EYE SINUS
EYE SINUS
EAR SINUS
EAR SINUS
EAR REFLEX
LUNGS
CHEST
BRONCHIAL
EYE REFLEX
PARA-THYROIDS AND THYROIDS
STOMACH
PANCREAS
SPINAL COLUMN
THYMUS
HEART
SPLEEN
CENTRAL NERVOUS SYSTEM
ADRENAL
KIDNEY
DESCENDING COLON
SACRUM
BLADDER
COCCYX
SIGMOID COLON
SCIATIC NERVE
PROSTATE
OVARY

CONSTIPATION

About four pints of hot water should be taken per day, as hot as you can manage. Pay attention to your diet and eat foods which have a high fibre content, eg., plenty of fruit, vegetables and salads. If possible, use pure olive oil as this helps to lubricate the system. Wholewheat bread should replace white bread.

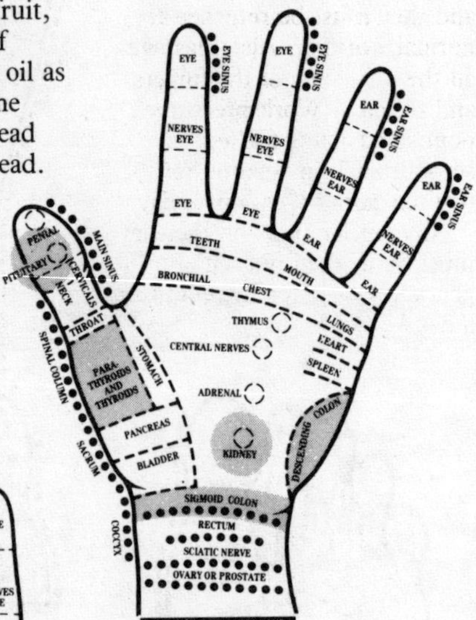

PRESSURE POINTS LEFT HAND

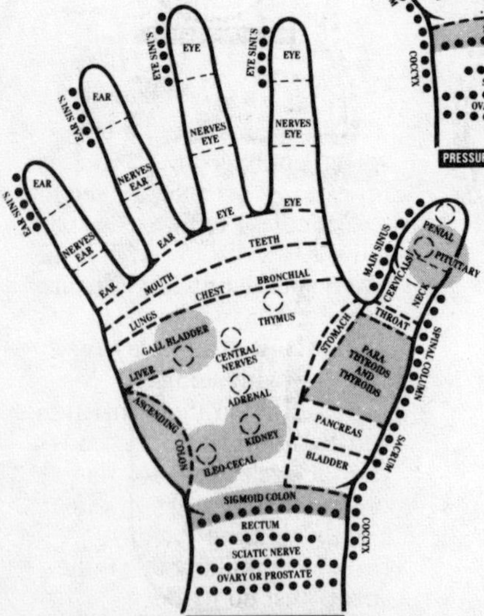

PRESSURE POINTS RIGHT HAND

Work on the hands and feet, treating the pituitary, thyroids, liver, gall bladder, kidneys, ascending colon, descending colon, sigmoid colon and the ileocecal areas. Any or all of these places may be blocked and they must be returned to normal working. Also massage all the top joints of the fingers and thumbs. Work pressure points and joints for ten seconds each in rotation for two ten-minute sessions a day.

Any tender spots on the ears must be worked out with gentle massage for five minutes a day.

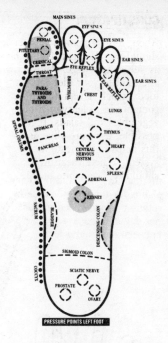

PRESSURE POINTS LEFT FOOT

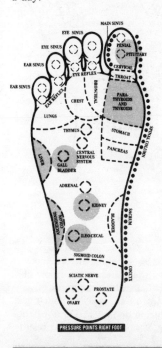

PRESSURE POINTS RIGHT FOOT

With the handle of a large spoon, apply good, firm pressure all over the tongue for five minutes per day. Also with the aid of a dry towel, pull the tongue out gently several times for a further two minutes.

You must also persevere, if you can, with stomach exercises. Hold the stomach in and count up to four seconds and then release it. Do this exercise as often as you can at any time during the day, indoors or walking down the street. Just do it. Be determined and persevere.

CRAMP

Use a comb clasped in the hand so that the teeth dig firmly into the palm for five minutes on each hand and rubber bands or clothes pegs on the fingers, thumbs and all toes for one minute on each hand and foot. Work upon liver, kidneys, adrenals, pancreas, nervous system, thymus, thyroids and pituitary glands for ten seconds each in rotation a total of ten minutes per day divided equally between hands and feet.

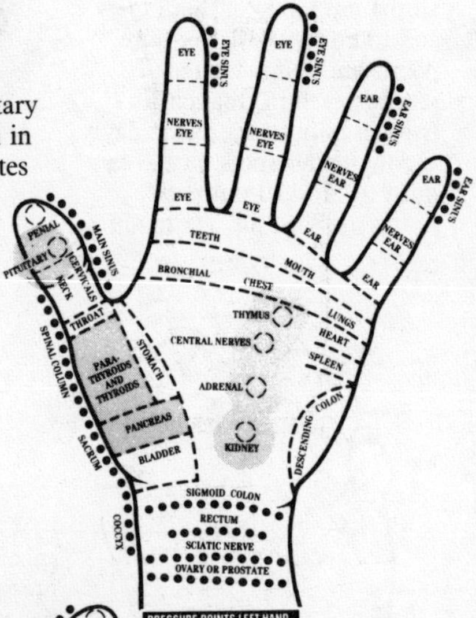

PRESSURE POINTS LEFT HAND

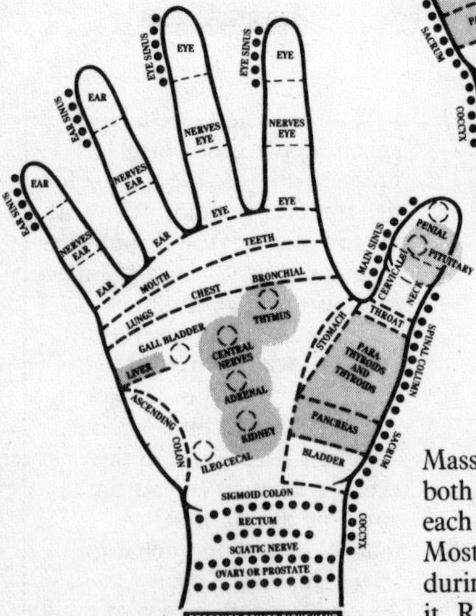

PRESSURE POINTS RIGHT HAND

Massage behind the knee on both legs and in the elbow of each arm for four minutes. Most of all, relax in your mind during an attack. Do not fight it. Relax into it for best results.

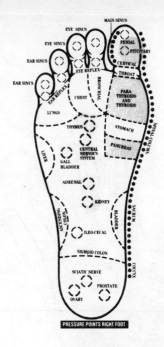

PRESSURE POINTS RIGHT FOOT

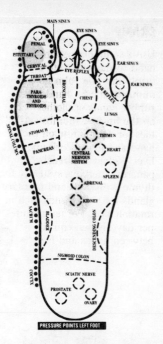

PRESSURE POINTS LEFT FOOT

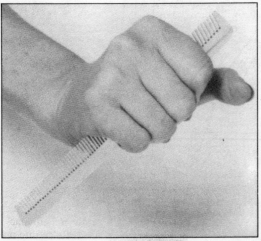

CYSTITIS

In this condition you will be applying treatment for an area which is badly inflamed. Work upon the hands and feet, massaging the kidney and bladder pressure points in particular. Work upon the kidneys gently for a period of, say, fifteen seconds, then go to the bladder and work there for fifteen seconds. Repeat this for about five minutes, going then

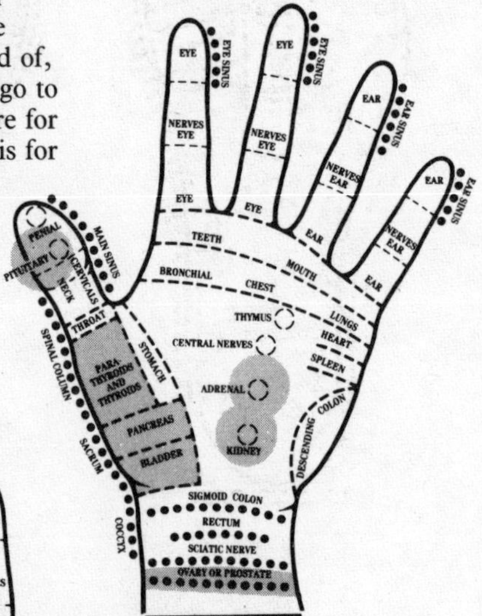

PRESSURE POINTS LEFT HAND

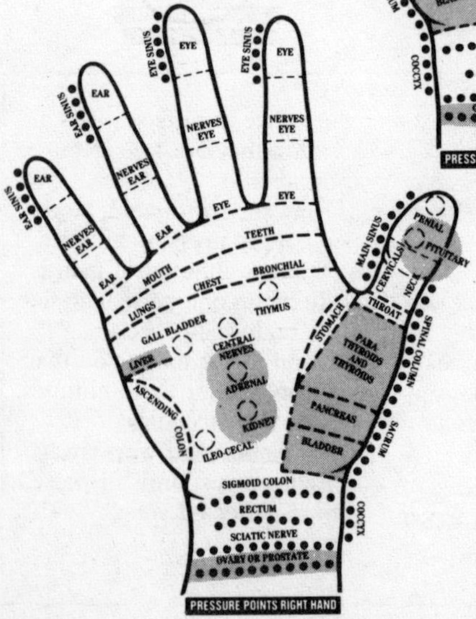

PRESSURE POINTS RIGHT HAND

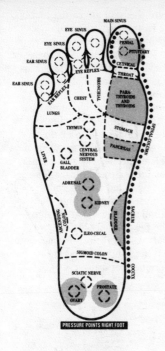

PRESSURE POINTS RIGHT FOOT

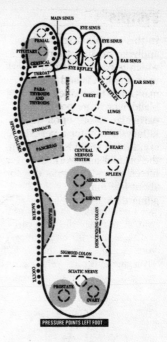

PRESSURE POINTS LEFT FOOT

to other parts. The adrenals, prostate or ovary, liver, pancreas, thyroids and pituitary areas also need some attention: work on them in rotation for ten seconds each. In addition, thoroughly massage all the top joints of the fingers and thumbs allowing ten seconds for each joint. Two sessions of ten minutes a day will bring great relief.

Work gently over the ears with the thumb and first finger for two five-minute sessions a day until they are free from tenderness.

Using the handle of a large spoon apply pressure all over the tongue, although if pain is felt to be on one particular side of the body, pay special attention to the tongue on that side. Do this for three minutes.

Have patience and determination and work away until all congestion is dispersed from the affected areas.

DANDRUFF

This is mostly caused by pollution in the atmosphere combined with sweat from the scalp. These create a scale which fastens itself to the scalp.

Be sure to wash your hair regularly and use a good, stiff brush daily on the scalp to loosen and remove all the dust and scaling. Also, every morning and evening, you should give your scalp a good massaging with your hands, or get someone else to do it for you. A massage like this can have a wonderful effect upon you. A good idea is then to rub glycerine and olive oil, in equal amounts, into the scalp. Make sure that you are eating plenty of fruit, vegetables and wholesome foods.

Rub your fingernails together for fifteen minutes a day. This need not be done all at one time. You could do it three times a day for five minutes at a time. The nerve endings to the head are all under the fingernails, so any massage of this nature is very stimulating for the scalp. Also press one set of finger and thumb ends against the other. This stimulates the blood up into the head region.

If you work in this way, you will find it will help you conquer dandruff.

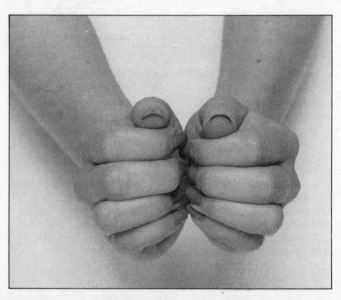

DIABETES

This is a condition brought on by the malfunctioning of the pancreas, so it is this gland you must concentrate on.

Treatment must be carried out on the hands and feet by massaging, most importantly, the pressure points for the pancreas, but also the pituitary, thyroids, adrenals, kidneys and all eye and ear areas in rotation for ten seconds on each pressure point for a total of five minutes on each hand and foot. Also apply pressure over all the top joints of the fingers and thumbs for three minutes on each hand and foot.

Using the thumb and first finger, massage all over both ears working out any tender places for one minute at a time twice a day.

With the handle of a large spoon, apply pressure over the tongue, from as far back as possible and forward to the tip for two minutes. Pay particular attention to the left side of the tongue.

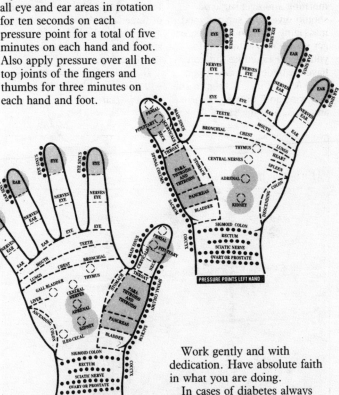

Work gently and with dedication. Have absolute faith in what you are doing.

In cases of diabetes always seek medical advice.

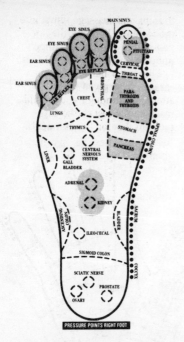

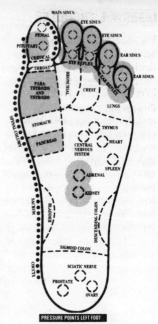

Labels (right foot): MAIN SINUS, EYE SINUS, EYE SINUS, EAR SINUS, EAR SINUS, EYE REFLEX, EAR REFLEX, PENIAL, PITUITARY, CERVICAL, THROAT, BRONCHIAL, CHEST, PARA-THYROIDS AND THYROIDS, LUNGS, THYMUS, STOMACH, PANCREAS, LIVER, CENTRAL NERVOUS SYSTEM, GALL BLADDER, SPINAL COLUMN, ADRENAL, KIDNEY, ASCENDING COLON, ILEO-CECAL, BLADDER, SACRUM, COCCYX, SIGMOID COLON, SCIATIC NERVE, PROSTATE, OVARY

PRESSURE POINTS RIGHT FOOT

Labels (left foot): MAIN SINUS, EYE SINUS, EYE SINUS, EAR SINUS, EAR SINUS, PENIAL, PITUITARY, CERVICAL, THROAT, EYE REFLEX, EAR REFLEX, BRONCHIAL, CHEST, PARA-THYROIDS AND THYROIDS, LUNGS, STOMACH, THYMUS, HEART, PANCREAS, CENTRAL NERVOUS SYSTEM, SPLEEN, SPINAL COLUMN, ADRENAL, KIDNEY, SACRUM, COCCYX, DESCENDING COLON, SIGMOID COLON, SCIATIC NERVE, PROSTATE, OVARY

PRESSURE POINTS LEFT FOOT

Massaging the pancreas

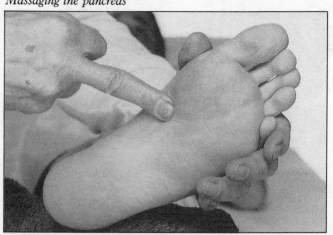

DIGESTIVE TROUBLES

For digestive troubles and acidity in the mouth, work on the hands and feet, massaging the pressure points for the liver, kidneys, thyroid, pituitary, pancreas, ascending and descending colon, sigmoid colon and thymus areas for ten seconds on each pressure point in rotation, though returning more frequently to any that are particularly sore, for a total of five minutes on each hand and foot. Also work upon all the top joints of the fingers and thumbs and massage down into the webbing between the fingers and thumbs for three minutes on each hand and foot.

The upper halves of both ears must be given special attention, although you should massage the rest of the ears too. Do this for two minutes.

Using the handle of a large spoon, apply pressure all over the tongue, from as far back as you can and forward to the tip, particularly in the centre.

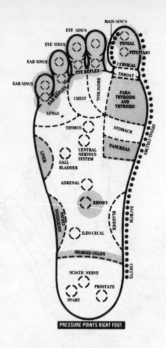
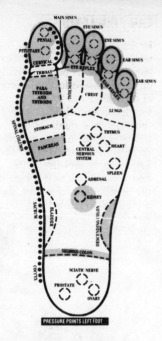

Concentrate on what you are doing. Do this for two minutes.

Indigestion can be eliminated by a change in your eating habits. Begin immediately to separate carbohydrates from protein. Do not eat potatoes, bread, rice or pasta at the same meal with meat, chicken, fish, cheese or eggs. You can eat green vegetables with fish, meat, chicken, cheese or eggs and you can also eat green vegetables with potatoes, bread, rice or pasta. So make sure you eat meat, chicken or fish at one meal and bread, potatoes, pasta or rice at another meal.

EAR PROBLEMS

In the case of partial or temporary deafness use rubber bands or clothes pegs especially on the third and fourth fingers of each hand and third and fourth toe on each foot. Apply them tightly enough for the tips to go blue for two minutes on each hand and foot. On the fingers apply pressure to the first joint and on to the sides of the fingers, particularly on the top joint of the third and fourth fingers. Alternate these for five minutes.

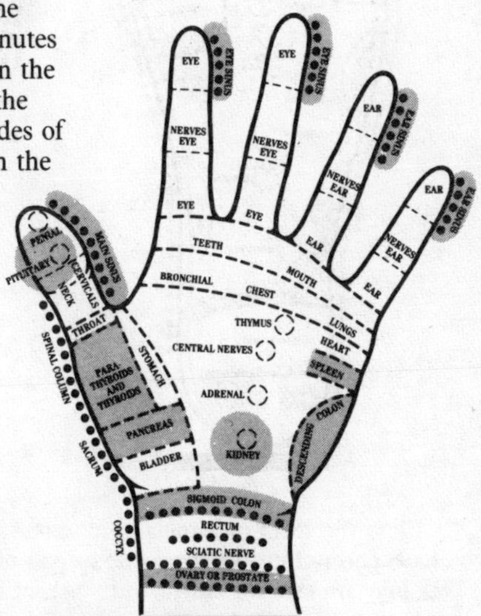

PRESSURE POINTS LEFT HAND

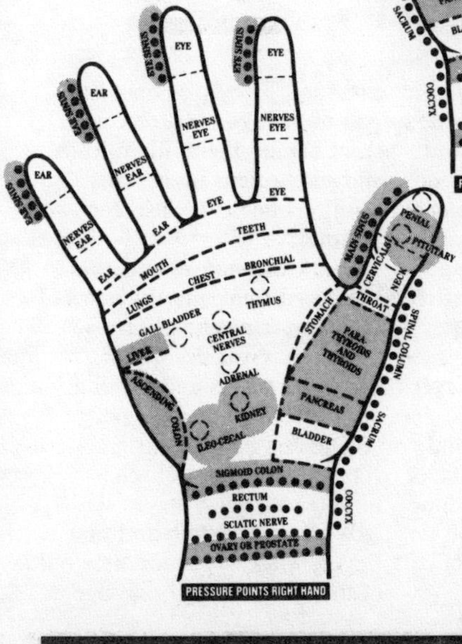

PRESSURE POINTS RIGHT HAND

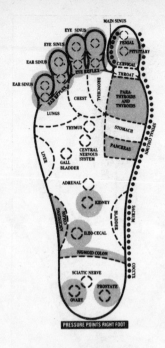

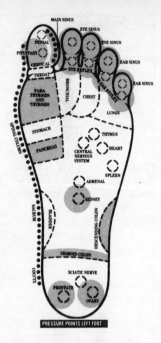

PRESSURE POINTS RIGHT FOOT

PRESSURE POINTS LEFT FOOT

Press the teeth of a metal comb gently into the finger tips for two minutes on each hand.

Use the tongue depressor on the side of the tongue nearest to the ear that is giving trouble. If you want results, work at it for ten minutes twice a day; that is all it needs. However, if your eardrum is severely impaired, it will never be perfect.

Pressure on the jaw behind the wisdom teeth can also be of great benefit. This can be done either by placing the thumb on the upper jaw at the back of the mouth and applying pressure, or by placing a little pad of handkerchief or cotton wool behind the wisdom teeth and biting hard on it. This position should be held for two minutes.

Work the sinuses and eye pressure points and the areas of the liver, kidneys, pancreas, pituitary, thyroids, spleen, ileocecal, colons and prostate or ovary. Do this for ten seconds on each point in rotation for a total of ten minutes a day.

With your thumb and first finger, work any tenderness out of the ear lobes and massage

the entire ear, back and front, for five minutes a day. Place your thumb in your ear, with the palm of the thumb upwards and the first finger on the outside of the ear, and massage gently with a rotating movement over the bony structure of the inside ear for one minute a day.

If you remove all the congestion in the areas I have indicated, your hearing will undoubtedly improve.

If you persist and dedicate yourself to this treatment, the results will amaze you. But you must stick at it. If you want success, you must be prepared to work and work and work. It is up to you. Remember that you cannot build up your body in five minutes. It takes a little while, and with this system you have to put in a steady performance every day. Have faith in what you do. Many people who have been deaf for years are now able to hear perfectly.

EYE PROBLEMS

If you are having problems with weakening eyes, use rubber bands and clothes pegs on the first, second and third toes, and the first, second and third fingers. When using the rubber bands leave them on for five minutes per treatment on the fingers and three minutes on the toes if you can manage it comfortably. Squeeze the first knuckle and the sides of the first and second fingers as firmly as you can for at least ten minutes per day.

Take your aluminium comb and place it on the tip of the first finger and apply pressure; then repeat with the second finger. Hold for five minutes, if you can, four times a day.

Gently massage the area where the nose begins just at the top corner of the eye; also

PRESSURE POINTS LEFT HAND

PRESSURE POINTS RIGHT HAND

massage the bony structure over the eye and on the temples at the side of the eyes. Do this four times a day for two minutes and do it regularly if you really want results.

Do not read in cars, buses, taxis, trains, aeroplanes, boats or ships. Rest your eyes

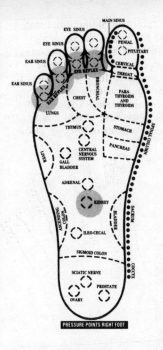

PRESSURE POINTS RIGHT FOOT

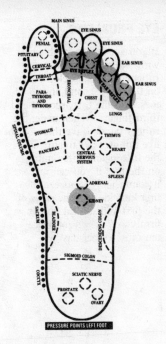

PRESSURE POINTS LEFT FOOT

whenever possible. If you can, always use daylight – as opposed to electric light – to read by.

Fill a basin with cold water and place a bright object in the centre of the basin. Keeping the eyes open, submerge your eyes into the water, keeping your eyes on the bright object, then look away, then bring your eyes back to the object. Do this for about five minutes twice a day.

Stand with the back of your head against a wall. Do not move your head but move your eyes as far to the right as possible and then back to the centre. Then look to the left and again back to the centre. Then look up, then back to the centre. Then look down and back to the centre. Do this exercise for about ten minutes twice a day. Also, whilst doing this exercise, look to the right-hand corner on the floor of the room. Then raise your eyes from the bottom right-hand corner to the top right-hand corner of the ceiling. Do the same to the left.

Always check the functioning of the kidneys if you have eye trouble and clear up any

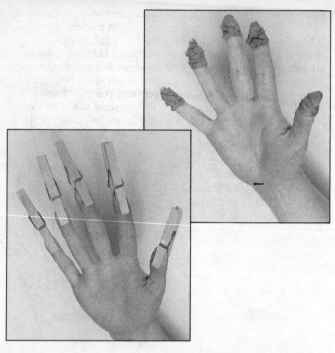

congestion you find in the kidney pressure point. When you work upon the kidneys, do one-minute massages twice a day. Find the pressure point for the eyes at the bottom of the second and third toes on each foot. It is best to work upon those areas with a pencil or something similar as it enables you to work over the pressure point much more efficiently. Do this for a period of three minutes twice a day.

Massage the entire top of both feet just at the point where the toes join the foot.

You need to work out all tenderness in that area. Work all along the line that extends from the back of the big toe right across the foot to the back of the little toe. This will bring back circulation to the eyes. A treatment of ten minutes per day will achieve marvellous results, whatever is wrong with your eyes, whether just muscle weakness, or glaucoma (a condition caused by a build-up of fluids which harden to produce partial or total blindness).

FATIGUE

When you are suffering from stress or feeling below par, you are usually physically exhausted and very nervy. Zone Therapy is the perfect remedy for stress, strain, nervousness and feeling below par.

Begin with the feet and give good firm massage over the pituitary, thyroid and parathyroid pressure points. Then go to the thymus area and massage in the same way. It is most important for you to free this gland from congestion as it helps to build up the nerve force in your body. If it

is malfunctioning it cannot do this. Then massage the areas of the liver, gall bladder, pancreas, kidneys, spleen, adrenals and prostate or ovary. Spend ten seconds on each pressure point in rotation. Treatment of the same areas and on the same time scale must also be given to the

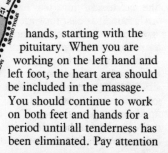

hands, starting with the pituitary. When you are working on the left hand and left foot, the heart area should be included in the massage. You should continue to work on both feet and hands for a period until all tenderness has been eliminated. Pay attention

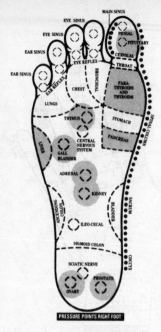

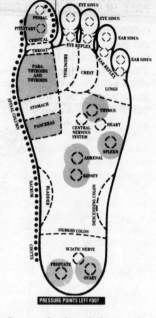

PRESSURE POINTS RIGHT FOOT

PRESSURE POINTS LEFT FOOT

to the top joints of all the fingers, and also massage deeply into the backs of the hands, working steadily and thoroughly and including the webbing between the fingers and the webbing on the thumb. Allow five minutes for each foot and hand.

With the handle of a large spoon apply pressure all over the tongue for three minutes.

Then work on the ears, beginning at the top of the right ear. Take hold of the top lobe with your thumb and first finger and begin a steady pressure right down to the bottom lobe. Complete the

entire ear, back and front and as deep into the ear as you can without too much pressure. Then apply the treatment to the left ear. Five minutes on each ear will give the glandular system a thorough toning-up.

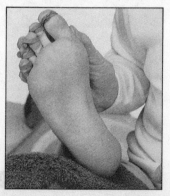

GALL BLADDER PROBLEMS

Gallstones form because the gall bladder is the body's reception area for bile. Zone Therapy has helped to dissolve gallstones in many cases. How this occurs we do not know, but it certainly does something to help the condition.

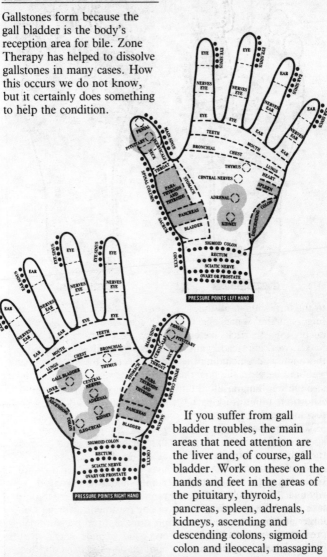

PRESSURE POINTS LEFT HAND

PRESSURE POINTS RIGHT HAND

If you suffer from gall bladder troubles, the main areas that need attention are the liver and, of course, gall bladder. Work on these on the hands and feet in the areas of the pituitary, thyroid, pancreas, spleen, adrenals, kidneys, ascending and descending colons, sigmoid colon and ileocecal, massaging

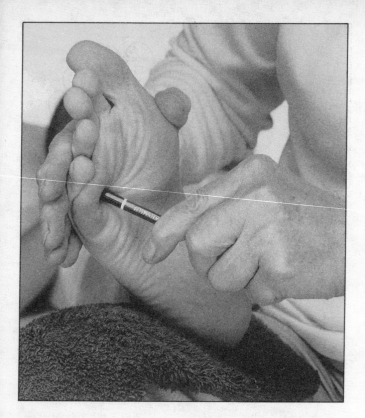

thoroughly to remove all congestion. When working upon the hands, also apply pressure to the top joints of all fingers and thumbs and also to the webbing between the fingers and thumbs. The elimination of poisons from the body and the balancing of the entire glandular systems is the goal to aim for.

You must proceed with care as too much massage around the liver pressure point can make you feel sick because you may be releasing stored-up poisons. So, to begin with, only massage for a few seconds at a time. Tenderness in the liver and gall bladder pressure points should be massaged carefully, so do not try to do it in one treatment. Moving from pressure point to pressure point every ten seconds, spend five minutes on each hand and foot.

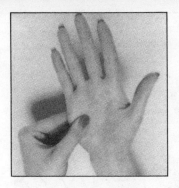

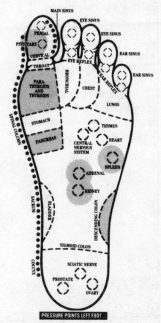

PRESSURE POINTS LEFT FOOT

Labels (left foot, clockwise from top): MAIN SINUS, EYE SINUS, EYE SINUS, PENIAL, PITUITARY, CERVICAL, THROAT, EYE REFLEX, EAR SINUS, EAR SINUS, EAR REFLEX, PARA-THYROIDS AND THYROIDS, BRONCHIAL, CHEST, LUNGS, SPINAL COLUMN, STOMACH, PANCREAS, THYMUS, CENTRAL NERVOUS SYSTEM, HEART, SPLEEN, ADRENAL, KIDNEY, SACRUM, BLADDER, DESCENDING COLON, SIGMOID COLON, SCIATIC NERVE, COCYX, PROSTATE, OVARY

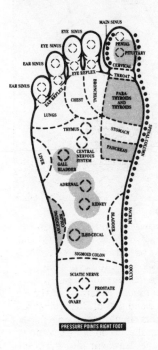

PRESSURE POINTS RIGHT FOOT

Labels (right foot): EYE SINUS, EYE SINUS, EAR SINUS, EAR SINUS, MAIN SINUS, EAR REFLEX, EYE REFLEX, PENIAL, PITUITARY, CERVICAL, THROAT, BRONCHIAL, CHEST, PARA-THYROIDS AND THYROIDS, LUNGS, THYMUS, STOMACH, PANCREAS, CENTRAL NERVOUS SYSTEM, LIVER, GALL BLADDER, ASCENDING COLON, ADRENAL, KIDNEY, ILEO-CECAL, BLADDER, SACRUM, SIGMOID COLON, SCIATIC NERVE, COCYX, PROSTATE, OVARY

Using the first finger and thumb massage all areas of both ears, noting any tender places, for five minutes a day.

Also, with the handle of a large spoon, apply pressure over the tongue, especially along the right side, for three minutes a day.

Make sure you drink plenty of hot water. Boil the water first, let it cool a bit and then sip it while it is as hot as possible. Have a cupful at a time, three or four times a day.

With the right attitude you will work wonders.

HAEMORRHOIDS

Haemorrhoids are painful veins that have become congested and protrude from the rectum, which bleeds and sometimes requires surgery. Zone Therapy can have a terrifically beneficial effect, so begin applying treatment without delay.

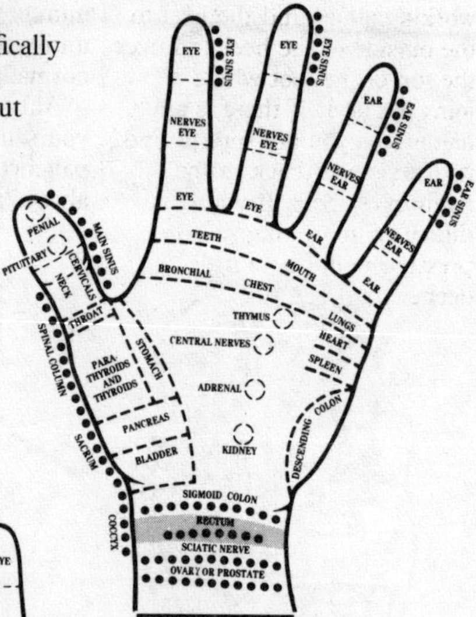

PRESSURE POINTS LEFT HAND

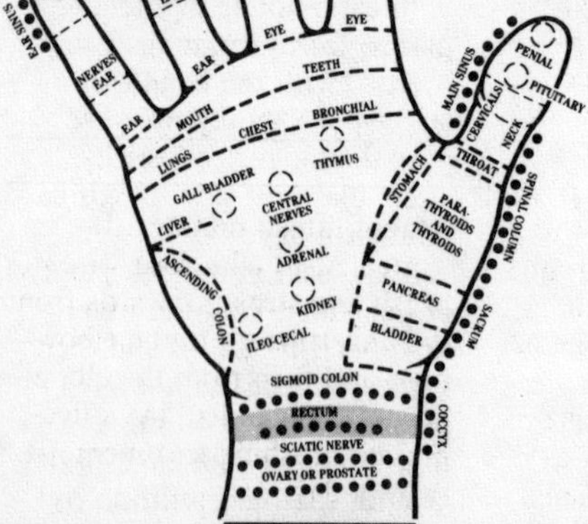

PRESSURE POINTS RIGHT HAND

Work your thumb as deeply into the rectum and haemorrhoid pressure points as possible and press in and down. Give yourself a good ten minutes' treatment twice a day, working all around the heel to the outside of the heel and over the top of the foot where it joins the heel. If there is any tenderness you are sure to find it. Keep going back to the really sore spots. If you have difficulty in locating the pressure point, go a little deeper until you do.

If you suffer from haemorrhoids or constipation, place your tongue depressor (the handle of a dessertspoon) at the root of the tongue and hold it. Try and give it a five-minute treatment twice a day until your bowels are acting normally.

All you must do is apply yourself to the task with patience and determination – it always pays off.

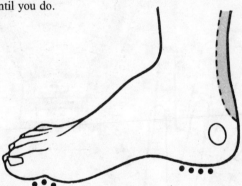

HAIR LOSS

Millions of people want to know how to stop hair from going thin and falling out.

Rub the fingernails together for fifteen minutes a day. Simply buff one set of nails against the other set just as if you are polishing your nails. Do it several times a day for a total of fifteen minutes. It works. Also, take your wire brush and stroke upwards from the fingertips up to the elbow first, and then from the elbow up to the shoulder. Do a five-minute brushing treatment twice a day.

HARDENING OF ARTERIES

As you grow older, your enzyme systems cannot cope with the abuse to which they are subjected if you are constantly eating the wrong kind of food. Therefore, if you suffer from this complaint, first you must correct your diet. If possible, cut out all dairy products, i.e., whole milk,

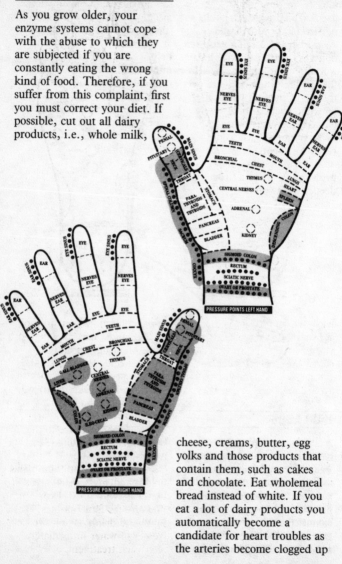

PRESSURE POINTS LEFT HAND

PRESSURE POINTS RIGHT HAND

cheese, creams, butter, egg yolks and those products that contain them, such as cakes and chocolate. Eat wholemeal bread instead of white. If you eat a lot of dairy products you automatically become a candidate for heart troubles as the arteries become clogged up

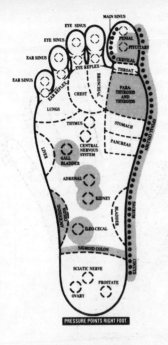

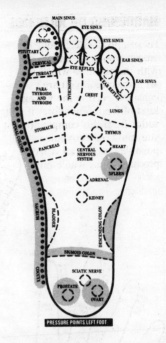

PRESSURE POINTS RIGHT FOOT

PRESSURE POINTS LEFT FOOT

with the deposit of fatty substances. If it is necessary for you to have milk, in tea or coffee for instance, then use skimmed milk. Make sure you avoid homogenized milk.

The treatment is to eliminate all toxins from the system as quickly as possible. To do this it is necessary to work on the hands and feet, massaging the areas of the pituitary, thyroids, liver, pancreas, adrenals, kidneys, spleen, gall bladder, prostate or ovary, ascending colon, descending colon, sigmoid colon, ileocecal, the cervicals and all areas of the spinal column. When working on the hands, massage the top joints of all fingers and thumbs. Spending ten seconds on each pressure point and joint, work on each hand and foot for five minutes.

With the handle of a large spoon, apply pressure to the entire area of the tongue for two minutes.

Finally, using the thumb and first finger, massage all areas of both ears with good, firm pressure for four minutes.

Always drink one or two glasses of water immediately after each treatment.

HEADACHE AND MIGRAINE

These disorders can have many causes: troubles in the cervicals in the neck, or in any part of the spinal column, in the sinus areas, the eyes, ears, pituitary gland, liver, kidneys, gall bladder, spleen, pancreas or adrenals, or they may be caused by constipation. Also hypoglycaemia (low blood sugar) may cause constant headaches and feelings of depression. Whatever the cause, the treatment is as follows.

Take your thumb and, opening your mouth wide, place it on the roof of your mouth. Apply pressure, trying to get it right under the spot where the headache is. If, for instance, it is under your eyes, then just at the back of the front teeth is where you would put the pressure. If, however, the headache is in the middle

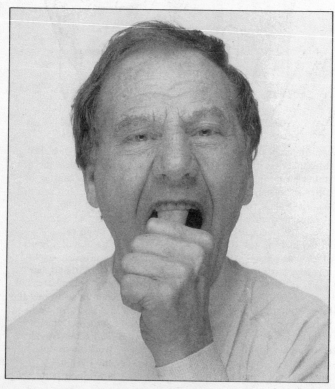

of the head, then you will place your thumb on the centre of the roof of your mouth just below the pain. This is a quick way of relieving the headache.

Working on both the hands and feet, massage the areas of the pituitary gland, the thyroids and parathyroids, the pancreas, adrenals, gall

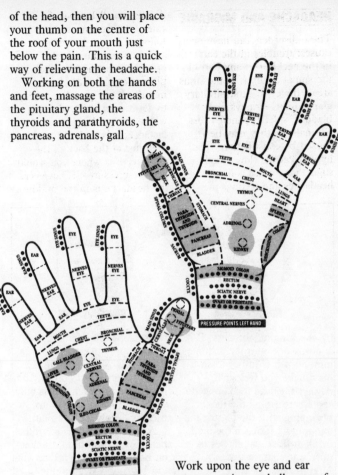

bladder, liver, kidneys, spleen, ileocecal, all colons and the prostate or ovary. Further, all sinus areas must be massaged and cleared, together with the lung and bronchial regions.

Work upon the eye and ear pressure points and all areas of the spinal column including the cervicals. Any of these could be causing your migraine or headaches, so find any tender places and work them out. Make sure the liver in particular is working perfectly

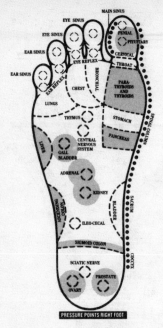

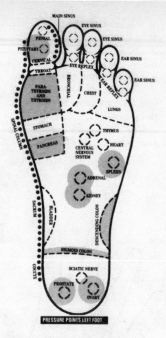

PRESSURE POINTS RIGHT FOOT | **PRESSURE POINTS LEFT FOOT**

by checking for soreness. If it is not, work on it for just one minute; if it is full of toxin it may make you feel sick. Always massage the connecting spots between all the toes beginning with the big toe for one minute for each toe, and drink at least two glasses of pure water afterwards. Migraines do yield to this treatment. Work all these pressure points for ten seconds each in rotation for a total of five minutes in each hand and foot.

Work over all areas of the ears with the thumb and first finger for five minutes and, with the handle of a large spoon, apply pressure all over the tongue for three minutes.

If you are able to do so, you must exercise, even if it is only walking. Get your head up, breathe deeply and step out.

Apply clothes pegs or rubber bands over thumbs and fingers on both hands as tightly as you can bear for a two-minute period, then take the clothes pegs and rubber bands off, wait for about five minutes, and put them on again for a further two minutes. Do the same for the toes, especially the big toes. Do this three times a day.

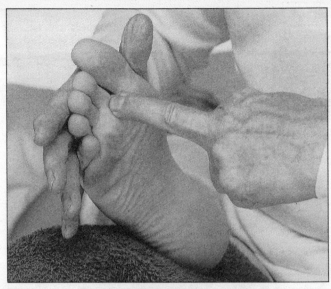

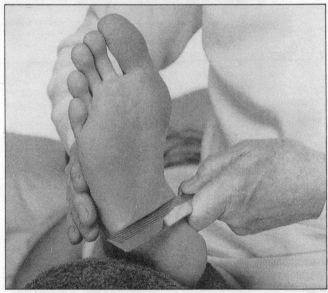

HEART CONDITIONS

Taking your heart for granted is a great mistake. Zone Therapy is, without a doubt, one way to prevent a heart attack. Zone Therapy can give you a clear indication of heart trouble, so if you are experiencing any discomfort it is very important that you learn to work on the heart pressure points without delay and so take preventative measures. Press your thumb in on the pad of the little toe, left side, and notice the degree of tenderness and congestion. Start work immediately, for further delay could eventually lead to a heart attack. Work out tenderness in two sessions of ten minutes a day, divided equally between hands and feet. The heart pressure point is buried deep in the chest cavity, so if your thumb is not strong enough to locate the tenderness use a pencil. Work also slightly to the left of the chest area and look for tenderness in the second, third and fourth zones of the left foot.

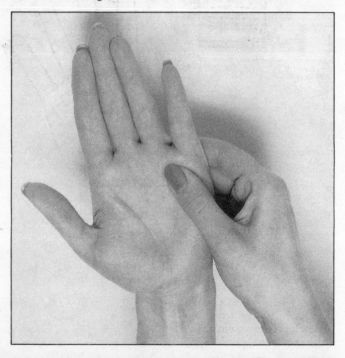

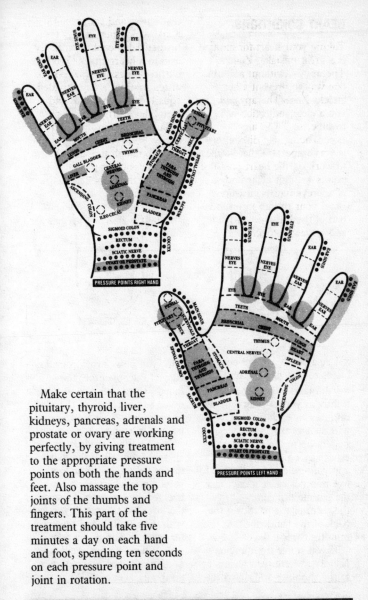

Make certain that the pituitary, thyroid, liver, kidneys, pancreas, adrenals and prostate or ovary are working perfectly, by giving treatment to the appropriate pressure points on both the hands and feet. Also massage the top joints of the thumbs and fingers. This part of the treatment should take five minutes a day on each hand and foot, spending ten seconds on each pressure point and joint in rotation.

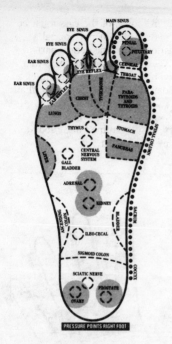

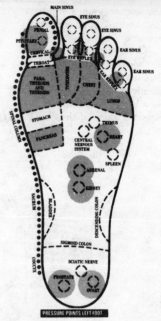

PRESSURE POINTS RIGHT FOOT

PRESSURE POINTS LEFT FOOT

Use a comb and rubber bands on the first, second and third fingers of each hand as tightly as you can bear for two minutes on each hand. Use a wire hair brush from the fingers up to the shoulders, especially on the left side, applying quick even strokes for five minutes twice a day. Use the aluminium comb all over the palm of the hand, on the back of the hand, for five minutes twice a day.

If you suffer from angina pectoris, where pain shoots up to the shoulder and down the arm, you must work from the base of the small toe, the fourth, third and second toes, down to the centre of the heart pressure point. Give five-minute treatments twice a day.

For shoulder pains, massage all along the top of the foot where the toes join the foot, paying special attention to the back of the little toe. Massage that area as strongly as you can with your thumb and fingers for two five-minute sessions a day. When all pain eventually goes, don't start to exercise or do things to excess. Remember the warnings signs you have had and use your common sense.

Work must be done upon the tongue, especially on the left side, by applying very gentle pressure with the handle of a large spoon for two sessions a day of three minutes each.

All areas of the ears must be massaged, but pay special attention to the centre part. Work out any tenderness that you can find for five minutes a day. Never work for more than five minutes on the feet or hands, ears or tongue.

Be determined and, above all, be patient.

Massaging the heart

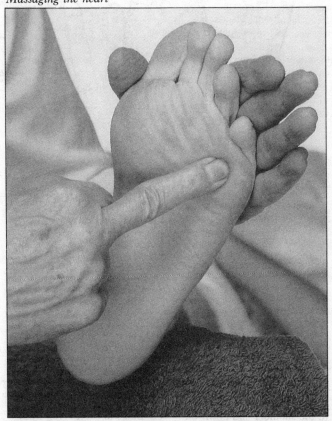

INFERTILITY

Infertility may often be caused by an unbalanced supply of hormones to the reproductive organs. This can apply to both men and women. If the pituitary gland is malfunctioning, this usually means that the thyroids and parathyroids are doing the same. This will eventually affect the adrenal glands, pancreas and reproductive organs – that is, the ovaries or prostate gland. Therefore a malfunctioning of the entire endocrine system is in evidence, and must be corrected.

Work must be done on both the hands and feet. The areas in need of treatment are the reflexes for the pituitary, thyroids, adrenals, ovaries (women) and prostate and testes (men). Also massage the top joints of the fingers and thumbs of both hands. This

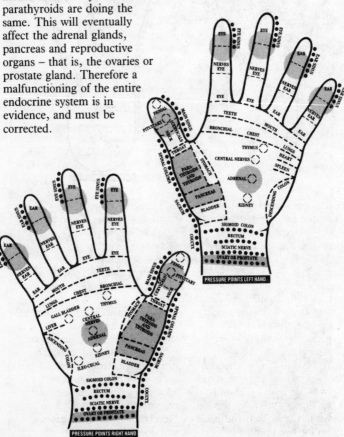

PRESSURE POINTS LEFT HAND

PRESSURE POINTS RIGHT HAND

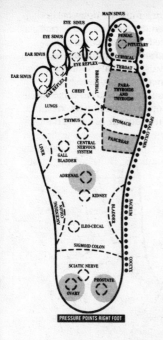

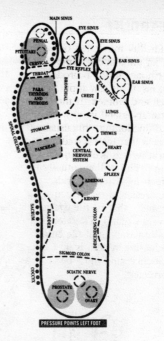

PRESSURE POINTS RIGHT FOOT

PRESSURE POINTS LEFT FOOT

part of the treatment should be practised for twenty minutes a day, divided five minutes between each hand and foot, rotating between the pressure points and joints every ten seconds.

Using the handle of a large spoon, apply pressure to all areas of the tongue, but particularly down the centre, for three minutes a day.

The entire area of each ear must be massaged. Use your thumb and first finger and work thoroughly from the top down to the bottom and back again for five minutes.

Whenever possible, do physical exercises if you are able to. Follow these by relaxation (see page 68). Put your heart into what you do, be sincere, and you will find that success will come your way.

If you show enough patience and determination you will succeed, unless, of course, you suffer from blocked fallopian tubes, uterus trouble or growths on the ovaries, in which case you must see your physician without delay. Nevertheless, in these cases still do this treatment.

INSOMNIA

If you suffer from insomnia, the subconscious mind has to be applied. This sounds difficult but it is actually quite easy. Practise by lying down in a quiet room and gently relaxing everything from the top of your head down to your toes, letting your mind concentrate on your stomach.

Do not think. Whatever you do, you must not think any thoughts. Just concentrate on your stomach as low down as possible. Place your hand on your stomach to help concentration. Do this for the first few days for ten minutes then increase to twenty. After one week increase the time to thirty minutes and, finally, to one hour. By following these

instructions, exactly as given, you will sleep.

You must work upon the pituitary, thyroid, thymus, nervous system and adrenal gland pressure points for five minutes on each hand and foot, moving on from each pressure point after ten seconds.

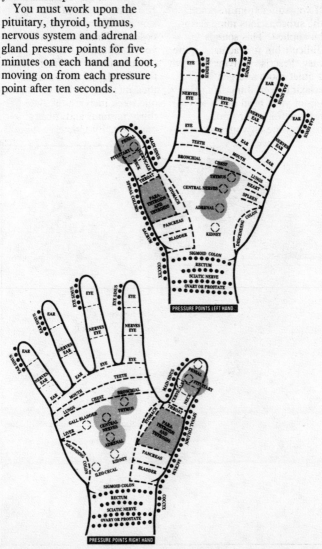

PRESSURE POINTS LEFT HAND

PRESSURE POINTS RIGHT HAND

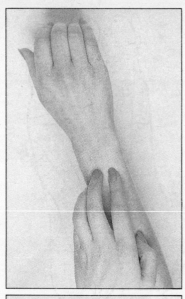

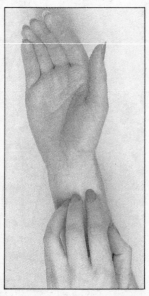

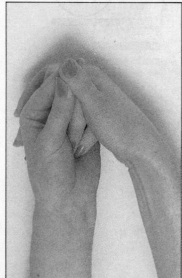

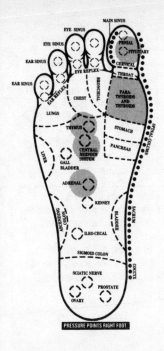

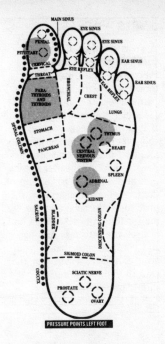

Insomnia may be caused by hypertension, worry, anxiety or emotional upset. All these affect the nervous system, which, in turn, automatically creates havoc with the glandular system.

Stroke your forearms on all surfaces with a wire brush, or with your fingernails, for a ten-minute period each day. Then interlock all the fingers of the two hands for ten minutes, pressing as hard as possible. Further, press the fleshy part of the top of your thumb (no nails involved) in the space between your eyes and hold for five to ten minutes just before you go to sleep.

Eat as much lettuce as possible.

JOINTS – ACHES

A great number of people suffer from aches and pains – especially, first thing in the morning, from a stiff neck or pains across the shoulders. How can you relieve that pain? If it is in the neck, look at the spot where the big toe joins the foot and massage that area as deep as you can bear it for five minutes. Then go to the top of the foot and massage from the little toe right across to the big toe for five minutes. Put a lot of pressure into this massage and you will find that, if you do it correctly, it will ease the pain in your neck and shoulders.

Rub your knuckles as deeply as you can into the soles of your feet for a ten-minute period.

If you suffer from leg cramps, massage deeply the cords at the back of each knee for five minutes a day and that will get rid of it within a dozen treatments.

If you have any pain in your elbow then massage the corresponding area in your knee for three minutes a day. This also applies to your shoulders and hip. If there is anything wrong with your ankles, massage the wrist and, in turn, if there is anything wrong with the wrist, massage the ankle. You will find it works.

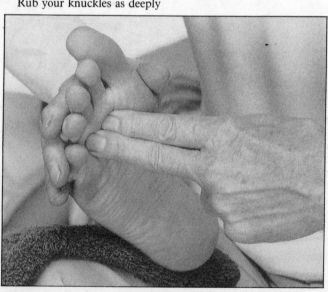

KIDNEY PROBLEMS

Look at your chart for the spinal area. Notice where the kidney pressure point is situated in the foot, then come across to the spine pressure point and work upon the area of the spine opposite the kidney pressure point until all tenderness has gone. Work must be done too on the adrenal and the bladder areas. This treatment should take five minutes a day on each foot, working on each pressure point in turn for ten seconds.

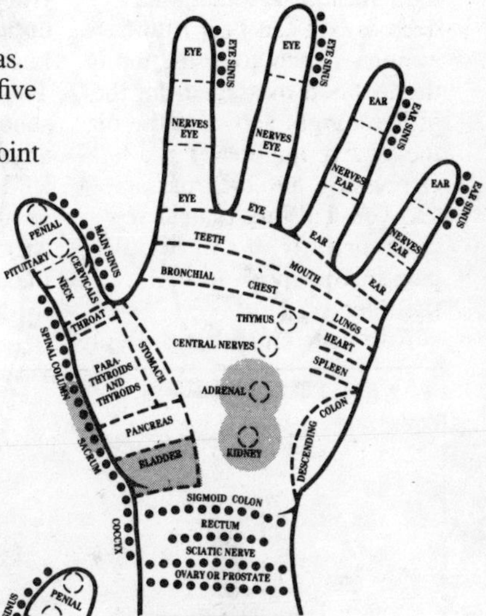

PRESSURE POINTS LEFT HAND

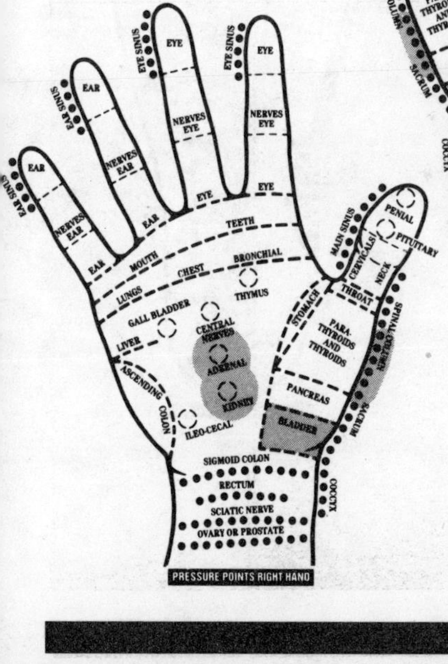

PRESSURE POINTS RIGHT HAND

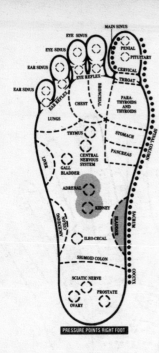

Use the aluminium comb on the palms of both hands. Place the teeth of the comb into the centre of the hand on the palm side, then put your fingers over the back of the comb and press. Hold for five minutes if possible.

Place rubber bands on all fingers and toes as tightly as you can bear for two to five minutes.

PRESSURE POINTS RIGHT FOOT

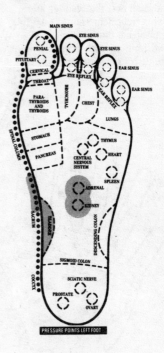

PRESSURE POINTS LEFT FOOT

LIVER PROBLEMS

Work upon liver and kidney pressure points, alternating every ten seconds, for three minutes a day.

Use the wire brush treatment, brushing from the tips of the fingers to the shoulders. First work on the top of the hand up to the

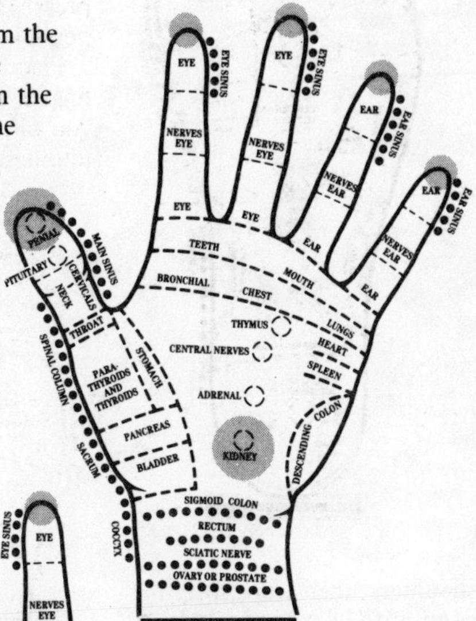

PRESSURE POINTS LEFT HAND

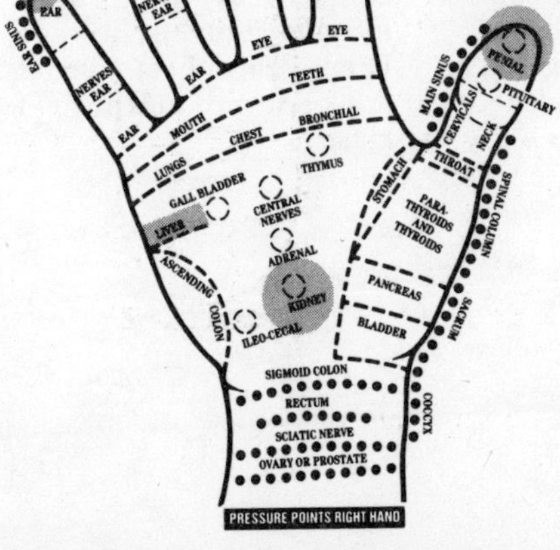

PRESSURE POINTS RIGHT HAND

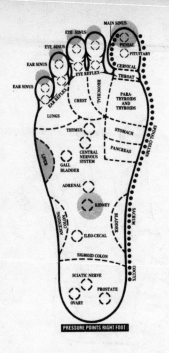

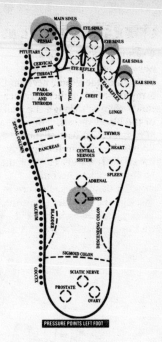

PRESSURE POINTS RIGHT FOOT

PRESSURE POINTS LEFT FOOT

shoulders, then work from the palm of the hand up to the shoulders. Do this for two minutes a day on each arm.

Work on all the toes and fingertips with a rounded pencil for five minutes a day on each hand and and foot.

Only eat one small meal during the day for you are trying to purify the liver. Drink plenty of hot water and drink skimmed milk if you feel hungry.

LYMPH GLAND INFECTIONS

The lymph glands are a network of vessels or nodes, situated in the groin, neck and armpits, which gather together fluids seeping through the walls of the blood vessels. They are a very important part of the body's mechanism for fighting infection. It is very easy for the lymph glands to become infected themselves. Be sure to massage the pressure point to these glands, which you will find in the feet, for five minutes a day.

MENOPAUSE, MENSTRUAL CRAMP, MORNING SICKNESS

Women seem to be the ones who suffer most in this world and not least among their troubles are the physical pains, complaints and discomfort caused by the female organs. Many conditions can affect the proper functioning of these organs. If there is any haemorrhage, do not use any massage treatment: immediately consult your physician.

Trouble with the ovaries can often be traced back to the thyroid, which is often referred to as the third ovary, so massage must be given to the pressure points for these glands first and then on to the ovaries and the thyroid glands. Functioning of the ovaries in women and the testes in men nearly always involves the pituitary as well as the thyroid glands. Massage of these areas will stimulate the ovaries, uterus and fallopian tubes in the female and the prostate, penis and testicles in the male. It is best to do this particular treatment with your thumb

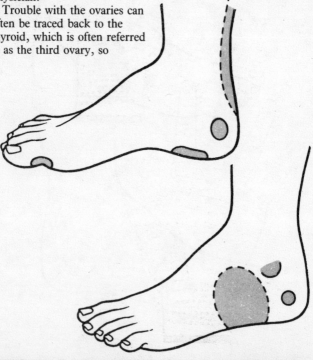

because of the tenderness you will encounter, if you do have problems in these areas. Work on pituitary, thyroids, pancreas, adrenals, ovaries, liver and kidneys, moving from point to point every ten seconds for a total of five minutes on each hand and foot.

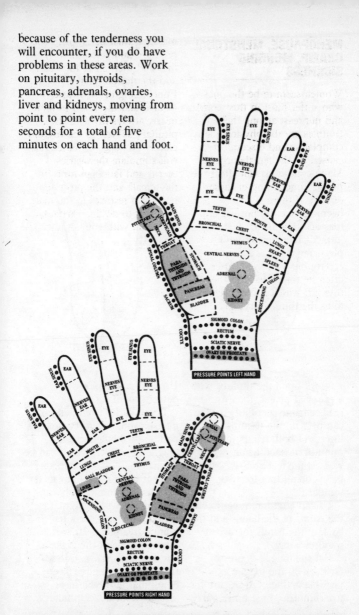

PRESSURE POINTS LEFT HAND

PRESSURE POINTS RIGHT HAND

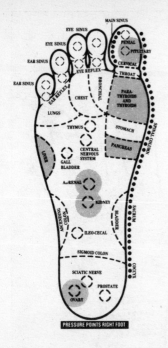

PRESSURE POINTS RIGHT FOOT

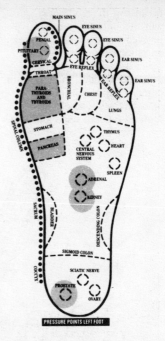

PRESSURE POINTS LEFT FOOT

Work upon the thumbs with a rounded pencil, then use rubber bands as tightly as you can bear on the thumbs and fingers of both hands for two minutes on each hand. Work well on the feet and use rubber bands on all toes for two minutes.

Use an aluminium comb on the palms of the hands and the back of the hands for two minutes a day.

Put the tongue depressor as far back on the tongue as possible and apply pressure for five minutes, three times a day.

Use the handle of a dessertspoon.

If you suffer from painful menstruation, then try this natural method. Use your tongue depressor, which can be the handle of a dessertspoon. Place it upon the tongue as far back as you comfortably can. Press down with a slight forward pressure for a ten-minute treatment. Hold it as long as you can, then take a few seconds' rest, and then reapply the pressure. Keep doing that until you have actually done a ten-minute

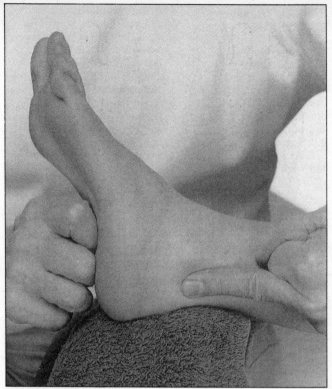

Massaging the ovaries

pressure, although the whole exercise takes fifteen minutes due to the little rests you are taking.

Do this treatment for three to four days before your period, twice a day, morning and evening, and you will find that menstrual pains will no longer bother you.

Do not use any of these treatments if you are pregnant, because they relax the muscles and the organs.

NAUSEA, TRAVEL SICKNESS

Work over the backs of your hands and wrists, either with your fingers and thumbs or an aluminium comb. Look at the back of your hand where the thumb and the first finger meet and work deep into that webbing.

Work right across the hand and work down as far as the wrist, then turn your hand over and work on the palm of the hand deep into the webbing between the thumb and the first finger and again work down on to the wrist. Give this work a ten-minute session then repeat until the nausea abates. Also work over all the top joints on all fingers and thumbs. Apply pressure to the tongue with a dessertspoon handle.

NERVOUS CONDITIONS

If you suffer from any nervous condition, it can be arrested and eradicated by Zone Therapy. Nervous conditions such as agoraphobia, claustrophobia, nervous delibity, anxiety neurosis, nervous asthma and stress and strain are caused largely by an unbalanced glandular system. If you have a shock to the nervous system, it automatically causes malfunctioning in the glandular system, and the way to eliminate this condition is by treating the glandular system. If you work upon the glands, they, in turn, will automatically revitalize the nervous system.

The treatment for these conditions consists of massaging the pituitary gland, thyroids, parathyroids and thymus pressure points. Also needing special attention are the central nervous system, the pituitary, the pancreas and the adrenals areas. When you have worked on these areas for ten seconds a time for a total of five minutes on each foot, go through the rest of the glandular system, i.e., the liver, gall bladder, spleen, kidneys, prostate or ovary, allowing another five minutes for each hand and foot. Then massage the top joints of the thumbs and all the fingers, and the webbing between the thumbs and fingers on each hand, for two minutes altogether.

With a soft wire brush give short, rapid strokes from the fingers, up the back of the hand, up the arm, up to the shoulders. Always brush upwards towards the heart. Do

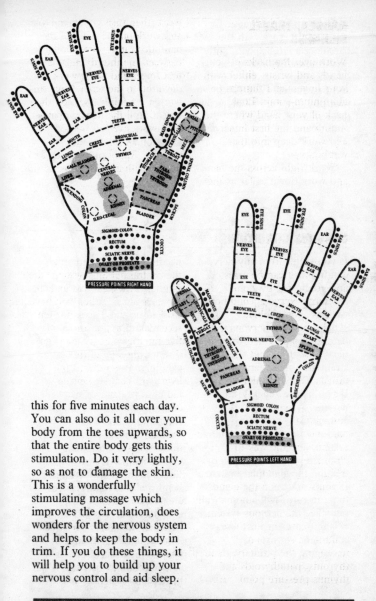

this for five minutes each day. You can also do it all over your body from the toes upwards, so that the entire body gets this stimulation. Do it very lightly, so as not to damage the skin. This is a wonderfully stimulating massage which improves the circulation, does wonders for the nervous system and helps to keep the body in trim. If you do these things, it will help you to build up your nervous control and aid sleep.

Work upon the tongue by applying pressure with the handle of a large spoon, and upon the entire area of the ears by massaging with the thumb and first finger. Give good, firm pressure over all areas for three minutes a day.

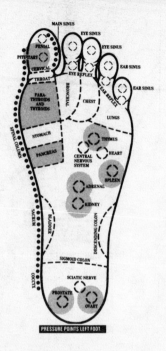

PRESSURE POINTS LEFT FOOT

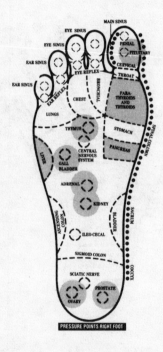

PRESSURE POINTS RIGHT FOOT

Interlock the fingers of both hands and squeeze as tightly as possible. Hold for three minutes, three times a day.

Place rubber bands or clothes pegs on all the fingers and thumbs as tightly as you can for two minutes for each hand and foot.

Clench the hands for three-minute periods as tightly as possible then relax. This is highly recommended and helps the nervous system.

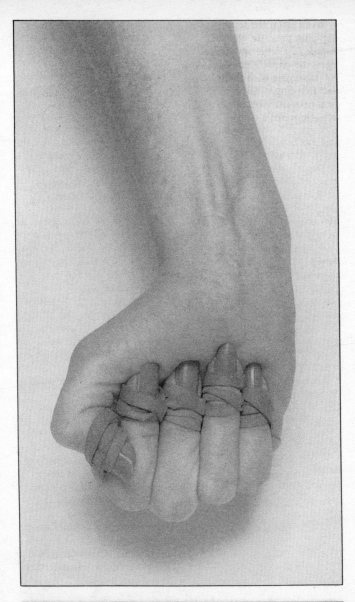

NEURALGIA

The first thing you must do for neuralgia is to work upon the entire glandular system, for a complete overhaul is needed. Work on every pressure point for ten seconds in rotation until you are sure all tenderness has been completely eliminated, then work across the pads of the hands where the fingers join the hands. You will, no doubt, find tenderness there, so persist over a few days, allowing up to twenty minutes, until all tenderness on both hands has disappeared. Now go down to the feet and work upon the pads of the feet just below the toes until all the tenderness has gone. Again allow twenty minutes.

Follow this by putting pressure on the tongue with a dessertspoon handle for a two-minute period.

Then place rubber bands on all fingers and thumbs as tightly as you can bear for two minutes on each hand.

NEURITIS INFLAMMATION

Neuritis can be very painful and immobilizing. If the pain and stiffness is in the shoulder you will work below the little toe on the sole of the foot and the little toe on the top side of the foot. If it is very tender, and it will be, then start with a one-minute treatment twice a day for two or three days, then gradually increase to twenty minutes a day in two ten-minute sessions.

Also apply pressure below all the toes from the little toe to the big toe. Do this on the sole of the foot and also right across the top of the foot for three minutes a day.

Then place rubber bands or wooden clothes pegs on all the fingers and thumbs over the first joint. Leave them on as tightly as you feel comfortable with for two minutes per treatment, three or four times a day.

Use a wire hair brush to brush from the fingertips to the shoulders of both arms for five minutes on each arm.

Also use the comb treatment on the palms of the hands, digging the teeth in for five minutes on each hand.

Drink three pints of hot water a day. Cut out any junk food or food that has a high acid content. This will assist in getting rid of the inflammation.

NUMBNESS

If you suffer from numbness in the hands or feet, first work on all the glands in the body, moving from pressure point to pressure point every ten seconds, and then rub the fingernails together. This should be done for fifteen minutes a day, not all at once. Do it several times during the day for two or three minutes at a time.

Also press one set of fingertips against the other set and really apply pressure, holding for five minutes. Do this five times a day.

Use a wire hair brush to stroke the arms from the fingertips to the shoulders; first from the top surface of your hand up to your arm to the shoulder, then from the tips of the fingers on the palm side of your hand up to your shoulder. Do this for five minutes. After that brush the entire body for five minutes. Do this morning and night to stimulate the circulation.

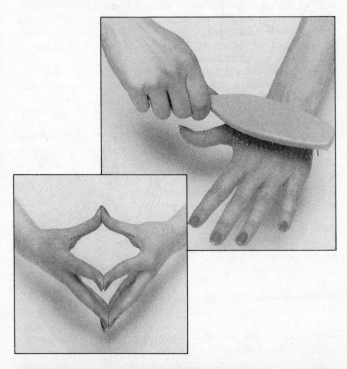

PARALYSIS FROM STROKES

A stroke usually happens when high blood pressure causes a blood clot in the brain. The nervous impulses to the affected side cannot be transmitted and so the muscles are unable to move.

Begin by applying pressure over all parts of the big toes and thumbs, particularly on the increase the pressure and time until you are spending twenty minutes a day.

Also work the liver reflex and the kidney pressure points alternately every ten seconds for two minutes a day on each foot and hand and work out any other tender spots you can find, working particularly over the entire top of the foot and where the toes join the foot.

Put pressure on all fingers and thumbs with wooden clothes pegs for two minutes a day on each hand and foot.

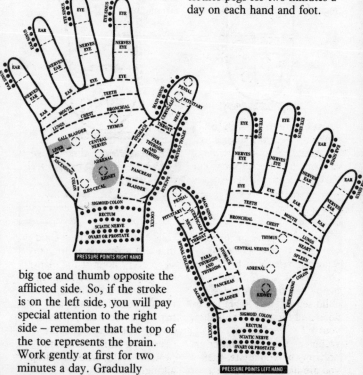

big toe and thumb opposite the afflicted side. So, if the stroke is on the left side, you will pay special attention to the right side – remember that the top of the toe represents the brain. Work gently at first for two minutes a day. Gradually

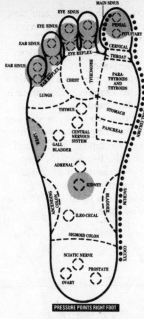

PRESSURE POINTS RIGHT FOOT

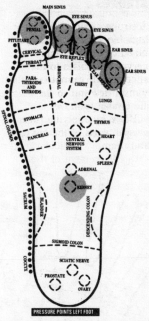

PRESSURE POINTS LEFT FOOT

Use a wire hair brush to stroke up from the fingers to the shoulders on the outside of the arm and then on the inside. Take five minutes on each arm.

It may take some time but keep working at it and you will feel the benefits.

PREGNANCY

When you become pregnant you must remember that the following nine months should be peaceful, tranquil and happy because your unborn child senses every vibration for good and for bad. If you allow yourself to get into an argumentative condition or an unhappy nervous state, then you are likely to produce a child that is nervous, a child that will wake you from your sleep every hour of the night, and give you a very hard time.

If, on the other hand, you remain peaceful, calm and happy, conversing in a happy, loving tone to your unborn child, you will have a happy, peaceful child, who will sleep all night.

PROSTATE TROUBLE

This condition eventually affects most men and is characterized by an increased frequency in urination (sometimes as often as every twenty minutes), and possibly by difficulty in urinating. These two conditions are usually a sure sign that the prostate gland is beginning to deteriorate.

An enlargement of the prostate means trouble, as it can cause pain and

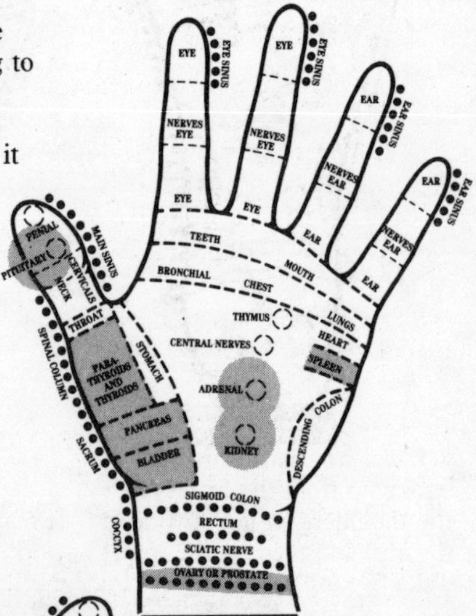

PRESSURE POINTS LEFT HAND

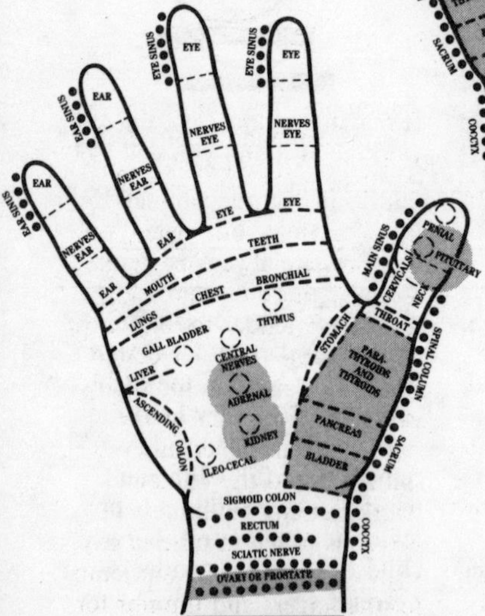

PRESSURE POINTS RIGHT HAND

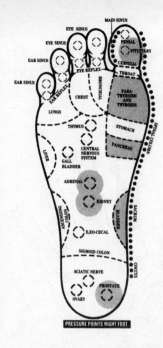

Pressure Points Right Foot

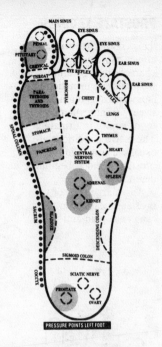

Pressure Points Left Foot

inconvenience, especially when it comes to passing urine. It is well to remember that it also affects the nervous system. It is the largest sex gland in men and it can and does turn a lot of men into nervous wrecks.

The treatment is to work on both the hands and feet, massaging mainly the kidney, adrenals, bladder and prostate areas for a total of five minutes a day on each hand and foot, moving from point to point every ten seconds. When working over the kidney area, be gentle and don't give too much pressure in the beginning. You can increase the pressure and depth over a period of a few weeks. Work a bit deeper on the adrenals and bladder areas, but, again, on the prostate always be gentle, because this area can be extremely tender to the touch. At the same time, check out the hands and feet for other sensitive areas such as the liver, spleen, pancreas, pituitary and thyroids, and work out any tenderness in sessions of ten minutes a day. Always massage the top joints of the fingers and thumbs for two minutes a day on each

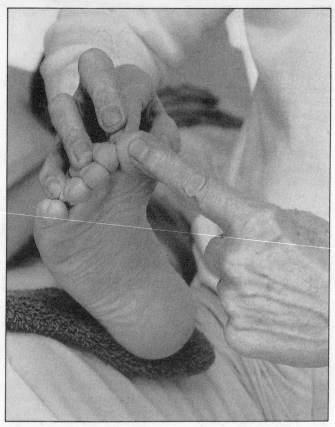

Massaging the penial

hand and foot. When you work upon the prostate pressure point, work the rectum pressure point and all pressure points in that entire area from top to bottom for two minutes a day on each foot.

Using the handle of a large spoon, put pressure all over the tongue from as far back as you can to the sides and front for two minutes a day.

Also with the thumb and first finger, massage over both ears. This part of the treatment should be applied for three minutes a day.

RECTAL PROBLEMS

Begin massaging the liver and kidneys and then the bladder. This treatment takes place on both feet, from the top of the heel, where it joins the foot, right up under the big root, which you find below the big toe. You must work all tenderness out of this area. This part of the treatment should be applied for ten minutes a day on each foot, moving from pressure point to point every ten seconds.

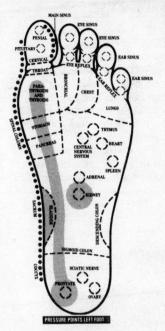

PRESSURE POINTS LEFT FOOT

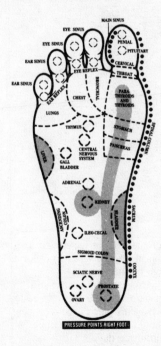

PRESSURE POINTS RIGHT FOOT

Then work upon the pressure point for haemorrhoids, rectum and prostate gland for five minutes – again only ten seconds on each point at a time. You must be persistent because, as you get older, a condition called 'prolapsed rectum' tends to set in. It is a painful and uncomfortable protruding of the rectum followed by very severe inflmmation and swelling. But, if you work at it, you may surprise yourself, for this condition can and does clear up.

RHEUMATISM

Work over all the major glands in the body – pituitary, thryoid, adrenals, pancreas, spleen, liver, kidneys and ovaries or prostate – for five minutes a day on each hand and foot, moving from pressure point to point every ten seconds.

Use a wire hair brush to stroke up the arms from the fingertips to the shoulders, first on the back of the hands and then on the palm side of the hands. Then do the same on the feet and legs. Always brush upwards. Work on this for ten minutes a day.

Take your aluminium comb, hold its teeth upon the palm of your hand and squeeze as tightly as possible. Start below the pads of the hand and put as much pressure on as you can bear, holding it for five minutes, if possible, then

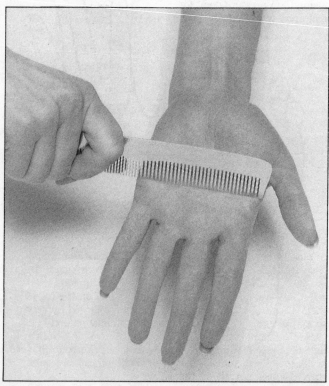

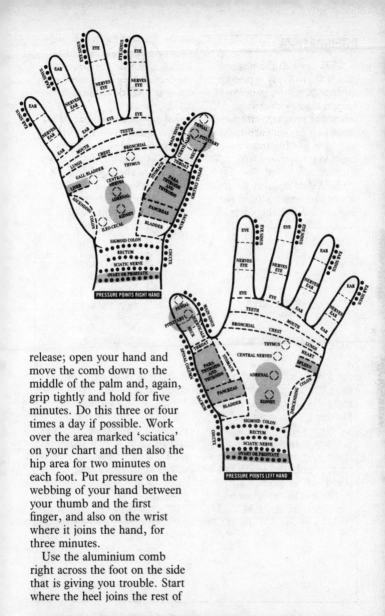

release; open your hand and
move the comb down to the
middle of the palm and, again,
grip tightly and hold for five
minutes. Do this three or four
times a day if possible. Work
over the area marked 'sciatica'
on your chart and then also the
hip area for two minutes on
each foot. Put pressure on the
webbing of your hand between
your thumb and the first
finger, and also on the wrist
where it joins the hand, for
three minutes.

Use the aluminium comb
right across the foot on the side
that is giving you trouble. Start
where the heel joins the rest of

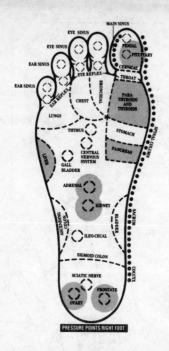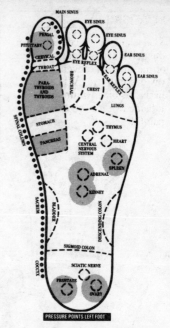

PRESSURE POINTS RIGHT FOOT

PRESSURE POINTS LEFT FOOT

the foot. With the comb across the foot, begin the pressure and work up towards the toes. Do this for ten minutes, twice a day.

Keep in mind that you are attempting to remove toxins from your body, so cut out all acid foods as quickly as possible. The three main acids are URIC ACID, LACTIC ACID and CITRIC ACID, found mostly in red meat, whole milk products and citrus fruit. Cut down also on eggs, cheese and tomatoes. Eat plenty of fish, honey, prunes and bananas. Drink skimmed milk. Drink at least four pints of hot water every day, morning and night. Take the JOSEPH CORVO PERNAMER FORMULA (see Arthritis, pages 96-97).

SCIATICA

The sciatic nerve comes out of the pelvis, runs along the back of the thigh and eventually divides into two. When this nerve becomes injured or inflamed, it can be extremely painful.

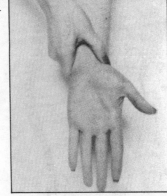

Sciatic pressure point

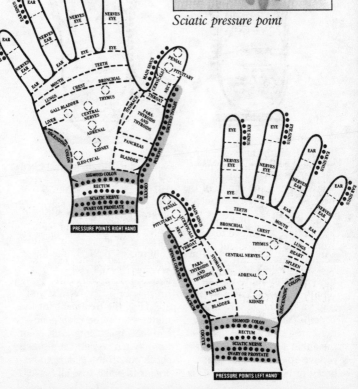

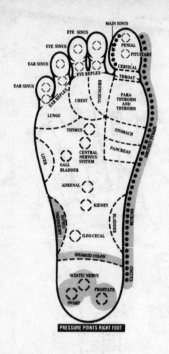

PRESSURE POINTS RIGHT FOOT

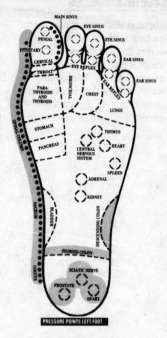

PRESSURE POINTS LEFT FOOT

The sciatic pressure point on the foot is situated slightly to the outside of the centre of the heel, so if you start treatment to the feet in the centre of the heel and work along that line to the outside of the foot, you will find the tender area. You may need something a little more penetrating than your thumb or finger, and I would suggest the end of a rounded pencil. You will find another pressure point on the inside of the ankle and this should also receive attention. The sciatic pressure point on the hands is where the hand meets the wrist. Work all the way across this area, using only your finger and thumb. In addition, on both the hands and feet, massage all areas of the spinal column, particularly the lower lumbar, sacrum and coccyx, and also the colons and prostate or ovary. Whilst you are doing the treatment for five minutes a day on each hand and foot, massaging each point for only ten seconds at a time, check out all the glands and organs to make sure all is well.

SINUS TROUBLES

For this distressing condition, go first to the feet. On the diagrams of the feet you will see that the main sinus is marked on the side of the big toe. Work over this area gently at first and then increase pressure after a couple of minutes. If you are suffering from a sinus condition, you

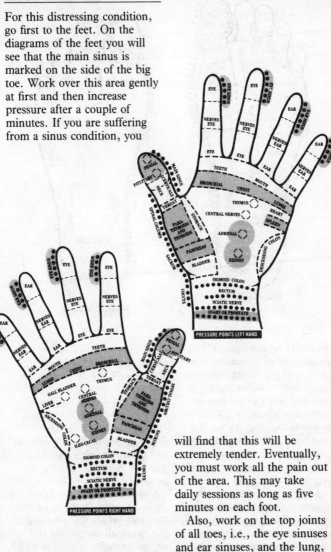

will find that this will be extremely tender. Eventually, you must work all the pain out of the area. This may take daily sessions as long as five minutes on each foot.

Also, work on the top joints of all toes, i.e., the eye sinuses and ear sinuses, and the lung,

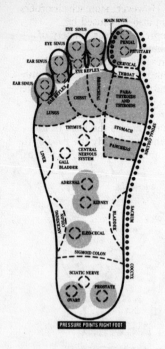

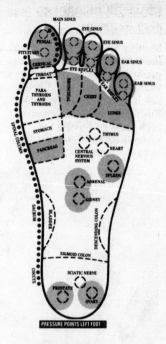

PRESSURE POINTS RIGHT FOOT

PRESSURE POINTS LEFT FOOT

chest and bronchial tract. This treatment should be repeated on the hands, starting with the main sinus in the thumb and working over the top finger joints and the chest areas. Make certain that the liver is working perfectly and that the ileocecal and colon areas are free from congestion. Then go over the entire glandular system, i.e., the pituitary, penial, thyroids, parathyroids, pancreas, kidneys, spleen, adrenals and prostate or ovary. Working on each joint and point for ten seconds at a time, allow another five minutes a day on each hand and foot for this part of the treatment.

With the handle of a large spoon, apply pressure all over the tongue and, with the thumb and first finger, massage all areas of the ears. Allow three minutes for the tongue and five for the ears.

Your sinus condition will improve tremendously in a very short time. Be determined and believe in what you are doing.

STOMACH DISORDERS (see also Nausea)

Start by applying pressure over the liver, kidneys and pancreas pressure points as your stomach disorder could be the result of bad indigestion. Do this for five minutes a day on each hand and foot – ten seconds on each pressure point in turn.

However, stomach disorders can also be caused by depression, fear, anxiety or emotional upset. So put pressure on the back of the hand at the base of the thumb and first finger for five minutes on each hand. Also apply pressure with an aluminium comb across the back of the hand, especially the base of the thumb and first finger, as this

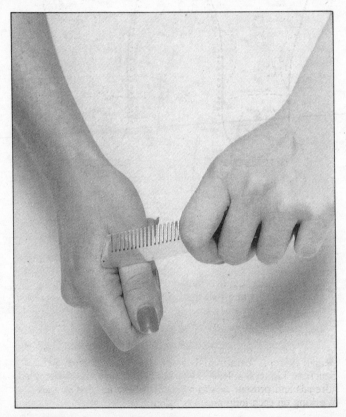

area has a vital link with the stomach and can bring swift results. Do this for another five minutes on each hand.

Work must also be done on the stomach pressure point.

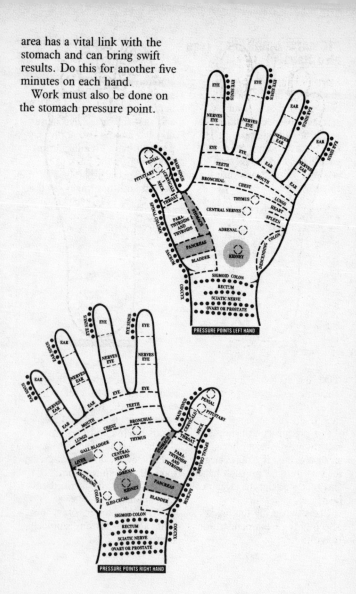

PRESSURE POINTS LEFT HAND

PRESSURE POINTS RIGHT HAND

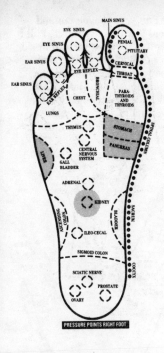

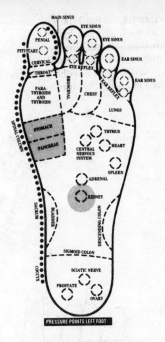

Work out all tender areas efficiently and quickly: you should allow two minutes on each hand and foot.

Put pressure on all fingers and thumbs using either rubber bands or clothes pegs for two minutes on each hand and foot – as tightly as you can bear!

Pressure on the tongue is also highly recommended for two minutes.

Use a wire hair brush and make quick, light strokes from the tips of the fingers to the elbows on both sides of the hands for five minutes twice a day.

Eat slowly; do not eat greasy food. If you suffer from diarrhoea, in any form, then eat bananas.

Drink hot water – say, four pints a day – for any stomach trouble.

THROAT CONDITIONS

If you have persistent throat troubles, first of all consult your medical practitioner for advice and treatment. Then you can help yourself tremendously with this treatment.

Firstly, drink hot water – as hot as you can comfortably take – at least five or six times a day.

Pull your tongue out and hold it with a dry towel. Pull it gently forwards, then from side to side and then round and round in circles. Do this for two minutes at a time. Then take a large spoon and, with the handle, apply pressure all over the tongue for a further two minutes.

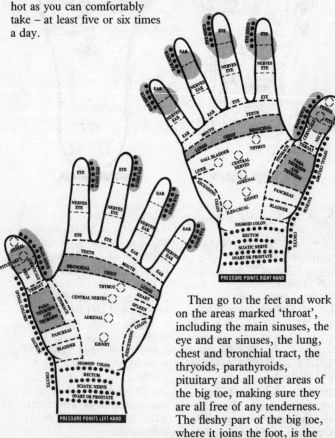

PRESSURE POINTS RIGHT HAND

PRESSURE POINTS LEFT HAND

Then go to the feet and work on the areas marked 'throat', including the main sinuses, the eye and ear sinuses, the lung, chest and bronchial tract, the thryoids, parathyroids, pituitary and all other areas of the big toe, making sure they are all free of any tenderness. The fleshy part of the big toe, where it joins the foot, is the

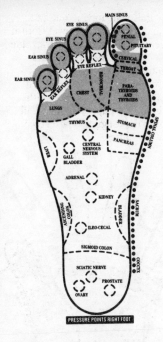

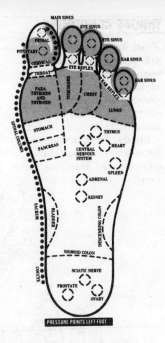

PRESSURE POINTS RIGHT FOOT

PRESSURE POINTS LEFT FOOT

pressure point to the throat, so that is the part you must work upon in particular until all tenderness disappears. The moment you put pressure on that area you will know that you are indeed on the pressure point to the throat. If your throat condition is being caused by a build-up of poisons in the system, that poison must be eliminated, so work on all areas as instructed. Work for five minutes on each foot, going from pressure point to point every ten seconds. Then go to the hands and massage all the top joints of the fingers and thumbs for two minutes on each hand.

With the thumb and first finger work over both ears from the top lobes down to the bottom lobes for three minutes.

Place rubber bands or clothes pegs on the fingers and thumbs and all the toes.

Take a mixture of senna-leaf juice and prunes. Stew the senna leaves, then strain off the juice and stew the prunes in the senna juice. Take twice a day. Remember that most throat conditions come from TOXINS, which must be eliminated.

VARICOSE VEINS

With this condition, the liver is the main gland at fault. Work upon the liver pressure point, gently at first, then increase pressure on a daily basis for two minutes. Also work over the entire glandular system every day for five minutes twice a day on each hand and foot, moving from pressure point to point every ten seconds.

PRESSURE POINTS LEFT HAND

PRESSURE POINTS RIGHT HAND